Compassionate and Free

An Asian woman's theology

Marianne Katoppo

ORBIS BOOKS

Maryknoll, New York 10545

ACKNOWLEDGMENTS

So many people have helped me and encouraged me in the writing of this book that it is impossible to mention them all.

However, I would like to acknowlege especially Preman Niles, Connie Parvey and John Bluck.

I am also indebted to Koson Srisang, for the title; Vincent Liyanage for the illustrations; and Aloysius Pieris SJ for his prayerful participation and spiritual guidance.

Second Printing, September 1981

The Catholic Foreign Mission Society of America (Maryknoll) recruits and trains people for overseas missionary service. Through Orbis Books Maryknoll aims to foster the international dialogue that is essential to mission. The books published, however, reflect the opinions of their authors and are not meant to represent the official position of the society.

Library of Congress Cataloging in Publication Data

Katoppo, Marianne, 1943-   *
  Compassionate and free.

  1. Woman (Christian theology) 2. Theology,
doctrinal—Asia—history. 3. Katoppo, Marianne,
1943-   I. Title
BT704. K37   1980   261.8'344   80-16368
ISBN 0-88344-085-7 (pbk.).

U.S. edition 1980 by Orbis Books, Maryknoll, NY 10545

Typeset in Switzerland; printed and bound in the United States of America

Table of contents

Introduction

Among the 500 or so classical Malay proverbs I had to memorize as a child, one of my favourites was this: *Seperti katak di bawah tempurung*—"Like the frog under the coconut shell."

The image was clear: the frog, never having escaped the boundaries of the coconut shell, could not but conceive of the world as dark, silent, limited. To this frog, it would be heresy to suggest that there actually was another world: one of light and colour, of music, and of vast open spaces.

Recently, an ecumenical team visiting a European country was told—jokingly, of course: "When everything is all right, use European theology. When things are going wrong, turn to German theology!"

For a long time, theology has been "European theology"; and for many people, "to be Christian" meant being a "European Christian". Any other way of being Christian is beyond them. The very same people who dance around brightly lit Christmas trees, and send their children to look for gaily painted Easter eggs, would denounce Asian cultural expressions as pagan.

Asian experience, being so different from the European, is also denied validity.

In Asia's struggle for a full humanity, women are specially concerned in moving towards a relevant theology. Asian women should be among the first to uncover reality—the *Asian* reality—and to cease being imitative of *European* theologians.

This book is an effort towards an Asian woman's theology. I do not use the term "feminist theology" because the word "feminist" has become too loaded. I am aware that theology, whether it is seen as a discipline or a critical reflection, is primarily *about God*. How do Asian women encounter God?

Perhaps we should reflect more on the words of one Asian woman who did encounter God:

Tell out, my soul the greatness of the Lord,
rejoice, rejoice, my spirit, in God my saviour;
so tenderly has he looked upon his servant,
humble as she is.

MARIANNE KATOPPO

I. Woman as the Other

By 1987, the majority of Christians will live in the Third World. *

The countries traditionally seen as Christian will no longer have the numerical advantage. Perhaps then we can finally relieve them of "the white man's burden". Perhaps we can finally assert our right to be different, our right to be *the Other*.

What does it mean to be the Other?

I speak from personal experience as an Asian Christian woman when I state that it entails a problem of great alienation.

Christianity, though Asian in origin has become western by adoption. Theology is in some places still considered to be the monopoly of European/German theologians. And in far too many cases, the Church leadership happily observes Paul's injunction for women to keep silent, but pays less attention to his conviction that all priests should be circumcised.[1]

In order to provide the context from which I speak, let me share my personal experience.

I am an Asian

More specifically, I am an Indonesian of the Minahassa, the northern part of Sulawesi, which the Portuguese mispronounced as Celebes.

Indonesia is a large archipelago, sprawling across the equator from 95° to 140° East of Greenwich. When projected over Europe there doesn't seem very much left of Europe.

The distance between the Minahassa, the country of my ancestors, where I was born, and Jakarta (Java) is around 2,000 kilometres: four hours by jet plane.

---

* I use the terms "First/Second/Third World" only for simplicity's sake. However, it should be pointed out that "Third" has often been misunderstood as "Third-class", "Third-rate", etc, while the original meaning (1956) of "Tiers" in the French expression "Tiers Monde" is primarily "the *third* person, who is not involved with either first (capitalist) and second (socialist), and who does not participate in the dialogue between the two." In other words, "Third" means "the Outsider", "the Other".

Unlike the other Greater Sunda Islands (i.e. Java, Sumatra and Borneo), Sulawesi lies in very deep waters. Its vegetation and animals are also quite different, and bear more resemblance to the Australian than to the Asian.

At school we had to learn about First Malays, Second Malays and so on, referring to various waves of people who came to settle on the islands at various periods in history.

The Minahassans were among the last. They came fairly recently, i.e. about a thousand years ago. The physiognomy and speech reveal a more northerly origin than that of other Indonesians.

Although it is all the same country, there are very great differences ethnically, linguistically and culturally between the Minahassans and the Javanese. Furthermore, the Minahassans are Christian (99%, the remainder being migrants from other areas), while the Javanese are predominantly Muslim (90%).

Historically, the Minahassa has had its own peculiarities. Four hundred years ago, after mass conversions carried out with great zeal by Roman Catholic missionaries, the Minahassa was under the Bishop of Manila—Spain being in control of the region at the time.

Two hundred years ago, the Minahassa chieftains concluded a treaty with the Dutch against the Spaniards. The Spanish had been bothering the Minahassan women once too often. The Minahassan men avenged their women by slaughtering a great many Spaniards at the village of Kema. Fearing retaliation, they turned for protection to the Dutch who were more than willing to oblige.

One of the most interesting clauses of the treaty is the solemn undertaking of the chieftains "henceforward to desist from the abominable practices of cannibalism and headhunting".

Around the turn of this century, the Dutch were seriously considering making the Minahassa "the Twelfth Province"—the Kingdom of the Netherlands had eleven provinces at the time. This gave the Minahassa a westernized image. The fact that many civil servants and a substantial part of the KNIL (Netherlands East-Indies Army) were recruited from the Minahassa did not improve matters.

After Independence, the Minahassa first became part of the State of East Indonesia. Then, in 1950, when the Republik Indonesia Serikat (United States of Indonesia) was dissolved, it automatically joined the present Republic.

I am a Christian

Less than 3% of Asian people are Christian. From a geographical point of view, the Philippines and the Lebanon are the only Asian countries with a majority of Christians.

Strictly speaking, I am a Protestant. The Minahassa was exposed first to the zeal of Roman Catholic (Portuguese and Spanish) missionaries, then Pietist (German), and finally Reformed (Dutch) missionaries. Independent since 1934, the church calls itself Gereja Masehi Injili Minahassa: the Evangelical Church of the Minahassa—which is probably the best name for it, "evangelical" meaning "based on the Gospel". It is officially classified as Presbyterian.

Protestant Christianity (7%) is one of the accepted religions in Indonesia; the others are Islam (85%), Roman Catholicism (3%), Balinese Hinduism, Buddhism, Confucianism and others. *Kebatinan*—Javanese mysticism—has not been accepted as a religion, although many practise it.

I am a woman

Numerically, women are a majority. Almost anywhere in the world, "women hold up half the sky". For example, in Sri Lanka they form 52%, in Indonesia 51% of the population.

However, in decision-making women are definitely a minority. In Sweden, traditionally considered to be one of the best countries for the representation of women in the decision-making process, statistics show that the membership of women in the *Riksdag* (parliament) does not exceed 21%.

Having come to Jakarta as a small child, I have continuously experienced *being the Other*.

At school, I was one of the few Christians among the Muslims. In the month of Ramadhan, our Muslim friends would fast, abstaining from food and liquid from sunrise to sunset. Indonesia is a tropical country, and I was much impressed by the self-discipline of my school-mates.

The Javanese culture is heavily influenced by the Indian/Hindu. They have an intricate social system which is reflected in their language and their life-style. There are different ways of addressing people, depending on their age and their status: young/old, inferior/superior, women/men. Raised in the Minahassan tradition, in an atmosphere which was much more egalitarian and less feudalist than that of Java, I felt at a loss not knowing the proper way of speech and style in the Javanese society. I remember my friends being horrified at the way I spoke to my sister, who is ten years older than I am. Fancy calling her by name, without any honorific prefix, and addressing her directly instead of using the polite third person! (I would ask: "Could I have a candy, please?" instead of "Would my lady my honoured elder sister be so kind to offer me a candy, please?"

My father was a great educator who believed in independent thinking and in The Historical Perspective. With regard to the first, as far back as 1949, he tried to propose a scheme for deschooling society—all the more interesting in view of the fact that he was the Minister of Education at the time!

Not having quite succeeded there—most people were still more interested in *schooling* society—he gave his undivided attention to the National Archives in Jakarta, and managed to uncover or discover an 18th century hero, Nuku Sultan of Tidore, whom the Dutch had pushed beyond the Historical Perspective. My father gleefully wrote a book about this man, who has since been installed in the Indonesian gallery of Heroes of Freedom in the history books. Although I was quite young at the time, this served to show me beyond any doubt that The Historical Perspective is there for those who can read—and write.

Independent thinking, when one is very young, is not always an asset. On 21 April each year the girls would have to dress up in regional costumes to celebrate the anniversary of Kartini's birth. After all, everybody knows this Javanese princess had served to bring the Light of Education to her oppressed Indonesian sisters. My father used to snort at my efforts to wear a sarong gracefully to school. He would point out that, firstly, the Minahassans' original costume was something quite ungraceful made of the bark of a tree; secondly, the first school for girls had been established in the Minahassa in 1881—when the good Kartini was only two years old in far-off Java—so one couldn't really attribute the coming of the Light of Education to her!

At the time, I wasn't ready to deflate the myth. Many years later, when a considerable number of people had reached the conclusion that perhaps this Javanese princess myth was something launched by the Dutch (I will elaborate on this in another chapter), I remember I wasn't too surprised. After all, I had already discovered that the ability to write, as well as to read, shapes history.

Thus my father taught me a lot about history. For example, that "Marianne" was the popular name for the French Revolution, a fact which greatly impressed my secondary school teacher. However, I did not know which and how many ingredients make up curry powder, something which would have impressed the majority of people, who held that a girl should be taught to cook rather than to think.

To sum it up, I found that to be the Other was an alienating experience: the Christian among the Muslims, the westernized Minahassan who was out of place in a Javanese society, the girl who was taught to look upon boys as equals, not as superiors.

The Indonesia of my childhood was subconsciously still strongly influenced by concepts of cosmic balance. People—even those in large cities—still think of themselves as being bound to one another by ties of common blood, common food, kinship and soil. The stranger, *the Other*, is the discordant note, the threat to harmony.

Fortunately, today Indonesia is moving towards the Great Society, i.e. the society where national consciousness is supreme, as opposed to regional chauvinist consciousness. In such a context, where "the Other is not seen only abusively as the adversary of Self, his/her Otherness does not lead merely to a dialectical play, but to an incessant putting into question."[2]

To be the Other, then, can be a liberating experience. One's Otherness can be used positively to enrich national culture, as has been evident in the revival of many traditional tribal elements, such as clan-gatherings, in the big cities.

But the social transformation moves slowly. The movement is from a traditional society subsisting mainly on agriculture and largely closed to outside influences, its members all being of the same blood and tillers of the same soil, to a society exposed to industrialization and secularization, its members not directly related or relating to one another from the comparative safety of *adat* (traditional) law and tribal society, and finally to the pluralistic Indonesian society. It's a complex and often painful process.

The Other

The limitations of this book do not allow me to go into the finer points of the theology and philosophy of the Other.[3] A few remarks will suffice.

God is *the absolute Other*, since God is eschatological; the divine Self is not given entirely to us in history, but only at the end of history.[4]

People tend to worship idols of their own creation: stones, trees, animals, human beings—and also systems, capital, cars, power. The prophets, in order to affirm God the Creator, had first to lash out against idols, or gods, created by people.

Sin, all sin, is by nature an all-encompassing absolute. When we sin we think we are all that there is and are therefore divine. We deny the Other and believe that our own totalized order is the kingdom of heaven. Or, as the old Malays put it, we are like the frog under the coconut shell.

From my personal experience as the Other, I came to realize that in the Church generally, and perhaps the Asian church in particular, *woman is the Other*.

Very few Asian Christians today believe that "God is an Englishman"; however, many have the lurking suspicion that, at any rate, He is a man (i.e. male).

All over the world and throughout history, the churches have tended to give male chauvinism not only a practical expression, but also a theological and even a quasi-divine legitimation, as Father Tissa Balasuriya said in *Eucharist and Human Liberation*.

If women are admitted at all to male-dominated institutions of higher theological education and/or patriarchal church structures, they are expected to theologize by proxy, faithfully to relay the ideas fabricated in male chauvinist (and often white supremacist) contexts. A woman's own experiences—of discrimination, subordination and oppression—are denied validity. Her personal encounter with God is denounced as heretical or hysterical: if the first, she is figuratively burnt at the stake; if the second, people hasten to find her a husband.

To get ahead in patriarchal society, woman is expected to become a man, i.e. to cease being the threatening Other. In politics—whether Church or state—we will often find that the few women who "reach the top" have often become so "man-ly" that they do the woman's cause far more harm than good. Some even become such dictators that some men will then say, self-righteously, that this only goes to prove that "women should never be given the chance to wield power"; they fail to recognize the underlying psychological process.

Many men are antagonistic to women's liberation because they fail to perceive that it is also *human* liberation. In fact, this indicates how deeply ingrained is their belief that woman is the Other. Man, being the Norm, is human. Woman, being the "deviation", is not human.

In the next chapter, I will elaborate more on the aspect of liberation. I will conclude this chapter by stating that I claim the right of women to be liberated from being the *threatening Other*. I claim the right of woman to be *the Other* in all her fullness and variety of gifts—*the Other*, who is *not* the adversary, the deviation, the subordinate of the Self, but the one who gives meaning to the Self.

If it is accepted that Asians should formulate their own theology—always mindful of the fact that there is no such thing as *pure* Asian theology*—why is it so difficult to con-

---

*The language of Asian theology is English, not an Asian idiom.

cede that Asian women may have their own insights to contribute to the richness of Asian theology?
>   I am — You are
>   I am free — You are free
>   But — *where* I am, *what* I am, You cannot be
>   Where *you* are, what *you* are, I cannot be
>   Am I encroaching on your freedom?
>   Are you intruding on mine?
>   Have I the right to be what I am?
>   Can we be fully human: You and I, each in our own way?

II. Woman's liberation is also man's

There is a saying: "Men of quality are not threatened by women's call for equality." These men realize that their worth as human beings is in no way threatened by women asking to be recognized as human beings also.

Men who feel threatened react emotionally, failing to realize that women's liberation is also human liberation insofar as it is concerned with the liberation of *all* people to become full participants in human society. Their reaction is caused by fear: fear of loss of status, fear of what will happen when patriarchal structures crumble—basically, *fear of the Other*.

The Church is a patriarchal structure *par excellence*. Through its unsound theology and ineffective ministry, it is undoubtedly part of the suffering of the women of Asia.

The theology of the Church has been oppressive and superficial not only with regard to women. Though Jesus is generally supposed to have been a carpenter, and his followers were mostly fishermen, we do not see too many working people in the Church today, except perhaps in rural areas.

The poor are hard to find in the churches. The Muslims, when they go to their mosque, take off their shoes before entering. So one doesn't really notice people who don't own any shoes to begin with. Many Indonesians go through life barefoot, a not uncommon practice in hot countries (Jesus and his disciples presumably wore sandals).

Many Christians—after all these years still faithful to the injunctions of Victorian missionaries—feel that one should be "properly dressed" when going to church. Of course one should wear shoes. My older female relatives tell me that before The War (the Second World War), one was supposed to wear stockings, gloves and a hat as well. In the sweltering tropical heat, the quality of Christian suffering must have been great indeed.

I had never been so keenly aware of this image of the Christian as "the person with shoes" until last year at the National GMKI (SCM) Congress in Ujung Pandang. A well-known professor—Muslim by religion—gave an excellent paper on Indonesia's cultural heritage, and the role of the student in preserving it. He remarked—jokingly, of course: "The main difference between you Christians and us Muslims is that you put on your shoes when going to church, while we take ours off!"

Religion is an intrinsic part of Indonesia's cultural heritage. Shoes aren't.

What is the image of Christ which Asian Christian men and women seek to emulate?

That of the bourgeois well-dressed, well-fed, well-educated, well-integrated human being?

Or that of the Asian labourer, compassionate and free, taking up the struggle against oppressive structures?

What is the Asian woman's image of herself?

Woman's self-image

The Asian woman's image of herself is fraught with dissatisfaction. This can be attributed to education as well as cultural factors. From an early age she has been conditioned to perform a subservient, subordinate role. Her status will always be derived, never primary. Instead of being a person in her own right, she will always be "daughter/wife/mother" *of a man*.

This has been so since time immemorial. Or has it?

In 19th century Europe there lived a man called Johann Bachofen, who wrote about The Matriarchy (*Das Mutterrecht*, 1861). He claimed that way back, far beyond The Historical Perspective of the male-dominated society, there actually was a universally matriarchal world. The people in this matriarchal culture recognized but one purpose in life: human felicity. And their culture was not bent on the conquest of nature or of other human beings. It was definitely *not* patriarchy spelled with an "m".

Of course—the 19th century being the age of conquest and exploitation—he was laughed at. His work was dismissed as being totally unscientific. So was August Bebel's *Die Frau und der Sozialismus* (published in 1893 and by 1895 already in its 25th edition), which had a few choice remarks to make about the power relationship between men and women. "Women have been coerced throughout history," he said, "women are the first slaves in history."

An increasing number of people uncovered evidence to support Bachofen and Bebel. They also had the infuriating tendency to write books about it, for example Louis Henry Morgan: *Ancient Society* (1877); Jane Harrison: *Prologomena to the Study of Greek Religion* (1903); Robert Briffault: *The Mothers* (1927); so that eventually some people came to accept that women have not "always" been inferior, subject and oppressed by men in their families and in society. There actually was a time, universally, it seems, from the beginning of the human race until around 5000-2000 B.C., during which society was organized on the basis of a gynocentric (woman-centred) culture. Matriarchy values were taken for granted, and the Goddess—not a male God—was worshipped.

It was later that male-based religion and philosophy started to play its part in demeaning and exploiting women—apparently so successfully that practically all over the world women still accept their unequal situation.

Words for women

In Asia, one has the beautiful saying (from the Quran): "Paradise is under the sole of mother's feet." In Indonesia, the original word for "woman" in the national language is *perempuan*, from the root *empu*, usually translated as "sovereign" or "saint" or "mother". In any case, it denotes someone of superior knowledge/skill/culture, as would be indicated in *empu Mada* (i.e. the Lord of Mada, also known as Gajah Mada, the famous prime minister of the kingdom of Majapahit).

Whether *empu* is to be taken to mean "sovereign" or "mother", it would at least indicate that the position of women was fairly high. In the kingdom of Majapahit, succession to the throne went both through the male and the female line.[1]

Other parts of Indonesia have also known women's rule, for example Bali and Timor. In parts of Timor there is an intricate system whereby the ruler, although a man, is regarded as a queen. Apparently a similar system exists in Thailand (see Appendix 1).

The fact that queens have reigned in various regions and kingdoms of Indonesia speaks for itself.

It is interesting to note that in Malaysia the word *puan* (from *perempuan*) has been retained to address a woman, whether married or single—the Malaysian equivalent of *Ms*, arrived at long before any such discussion in the West.

Language as an indicator of subordination

In many Indonesian tribal societies, a teknonym is used as a form of address. Hence, if one's eldest child is called Kamang, one would be either *Bapak* Kamang (= Kamang's father) or *Ibu* Kamang (= Kamang's mother), regardless of whether the child is male or female.

Traditionally, there was no concept of *Mrs* as understood in the English-speaking cultures. And the use of family surnames has largely been the result of colonial influence. The concept of private property was virtually unknown, hence there wasn't any direct or pressing need for family names.

Since the word *perempuan* was originally Malay, it has been regarded as coarse and not literary. It has become increasingly fashionable to use complicated words of Sanskrit origin, and lately, the word *wanita* has been generally used. This word, which to the best of my knowledge means "fragrance"—nice indeed, although one could think of more dynamic ways by which women might permeate the atmosphere—apparently became popular about the time of the Second World War. (For further discussion on language, see Appendix II.)

The famous Indonesian poet Ismail Marzuki wrote a song using the words *wanita* and *pria* (woman and man), both from the Sanskrit, instead of *perempuan* and *laki-laki*, which are the original Malay. The song itself is a hymn to the subordination of women. It says, among other things:

Ditakdirkan alam pria berkuasa,
adapun wanita lemah lembut manja.

meaning:

Nature has decreed that man should rule;
while woman should be soft, gentle, indulged.

It is still a very popular song. The Art Centre in Jakarta is called Taman Ismail Marzuki, "Ismail Marzuki Garden", after the great poet.

No monument of any kind has been built for Dewi Sartika, a great woman educator, who established a network of girls' schools in western Java.

Kartini

The Dutch spent considerable effort in having Kartini (1879-1904) acclaimed as *The* Pioneer of Women's Education.

It might be useful to have a closer look at Kartini. It can't be denied that she had some good ideas, not unlike Mary Wollstonecraft, who lived about a century earlier in England.[2] Like Mary Wollstonecraft, too, she died in childbirth. But whereas Mary Wollstonecraft wrote some very important contributions to vindicating women's rights, Kartini's legacy consists of her correspondence with Dutch men and women. *

It must have pleased the Dutch considerably to hear her plead over and over again: "Give the Javanese education... let us be like you", etc. It fitted in very well with their ethical policy of the time, that the exploitation of the "natives" could be supplemented with a little education as well.

Kartini's letters were carefully edited, so that for a long time readers did not know that she was in fact the daughter of a concubine of the Regent of Japara, not of the head wife (whom she refers to as "Mother"). Nor did they know that at 24, which was ancient in the sight of her contemporaries—on learning to her great distress that her younger sister was getting married—she consented to a polygamous marriage with the Regent of Rembang, an elderly man with several concubines.

Of course, one could argue that she didn't have much choice. Without being judgmental about Kartini, one wonders why these factors were omitted from many of her biographies.

---

* Some people actually think that Kartini wrote the book *From Darkness to Light*. She did not. This book is an edited collection of her letters.

Kartini's ideal image of the fully liberated human being was apparently personified in the Dutchman/woman, a mistake which many oppressed people have made when viewing their oppressors.

A few other women who were active pioneers in the Indonesian women's movement, such as Dewi Sartika, whom I have already mentioned, and Rahma el-Yunusia of Padang Panjang (West Sumatra), did not share Kartini's view. Rahma even refused government subsidy for her religious girls' schools (established in 1922), because she didn't want any undue influence on the curriculum. It is interesting that these women's substantial contributions to bringing the Light of Education to their sisters never received the same amount of attention or publicity as Kartini's.

The Indonesian understanding of woman

Indonesian society, like most Asian societies, is not so much achievement-oriented as relationships-oriented. If the woman, in this constellation of relationships, occupies a place of importance and interest, this should help her to be more assured of her own dignity and worth.

She need not actually be a mother biologically. In her relationship to other people's children, however, she can be a mother: loving them and teaching them. The same applies to a man.

Eminent—and patriarchal—anthropologists such as Malinowsky who regarded the individual family as the pivotal element of society, seem to have been horrified by the idea of collective motherhood. Yet it is a fact that in virtually all tribal societies a child will call its mother's sisters "mother". In the Batak society, for example, the mother's elder sister is *inang tua*, "elder mother", whilst her younger sister is *inang muda*, "younger mother".

The extreme individualization and alienation of the person, as may be the case in western society, is quite uncommon. If it occurs at all, it may be directly related to the rapid social changes which are not always for the better.

Women play an important, if not indispensable, role in the processes of production and reproduction. This is why women enjoyed such a high status in the matriarchal societies of old. In these societies—worshippers of the Goddess—sexuality, child-rearing and social organization were governed by communality and kinship groups, and not by a handful of *men*.

The matriarchy was by no means a mirror-image of the patriarchal society. It was egalitarian, not authoritarian. It was self-sufficient, producing for immediate consumption, not for surplus. Neither was it aggressive. Evidence for this is found in the archeological site of Catal Huyut, Anatolia. A neolithic matriarchal society, it shows no traces of violent death during a period of 800 years!

If women stayed at home in such a context, it was because at the time the home was the centre of power. It was definitely not the marginalized sphere it has become in many patriarchal societies, where it is the place women are confined to so that they may devote their whole life to the nurture of men and children.

The position of women became progressively worse in societies that had abandoned the matriarchy. In ancient Sumer, for example, a man was put to death for rape. Compare that to the Mosaic law where, if the woman was lucky, she got to marry the rapist. If not, she was stoned to death.

Throughout thousands of years of conditioning, woman's self-image also deteriorated. From the exalted, the sovereign, the mother, she became the slave and the sex object.

In the case of Christian women, this is also the result of the earlier mentioned tendency of the churches to give male chauvinism a theological and quasi-divine legitimation.

There are churches where women have no awareness of being created in the image of God, *imago Dei*. They have always been taught that woman was created only to be "a helper" unto man, the churches conveniently overlooking the implications of the Hebrew *'ezer* (translated "helper"), which is otherwise used for God, the Help of the Helpless.

The image of Asian woman, projected through the mass media in Asia today, is often a faithful copy of her western sister: the bourgeois housewife. In Sri Lanka, we see evidence of this in the comparison of advertisements for the English-language newspaper with those for the Sinhalese/Tamil papers. Often the pictures are exactly the same, except that in the English paper she wears a dress; in the Sinhalese/Tamil she wears a sari. In both papers she marvels at the wonders of modern technology, such as water-softeners or bathroom tiles.

Even in patriarchal societies like the Karo Batak there are folk-tales that witness to a different kind of woman, for example Putri Ijo (Princess Green), and Beru Ginting Pase (Daughter of Ginting Pase). The latter illustrates the plight of a woman who was unfortunate enough to lack male protectors. Her father died, and since she had no brothers the whole inheritance went to her uncle, who promptly sold her off as a slave. Through her courage and her endurance she managed to return later with a small army and take revenge on the wicked uncle.

In the Minahassa, there is the story of the beautiful Pingkan Mogogunoi, who is said to have had such a delicate fair skin that when she swallowed the liquid of the betel nut, one could watch it going down her throat! The king of the neighbouring region of Bolaang Mongondow fell in love with Pingkan, and came to abduct her with his army. She managed to persuade him to put on her husband's clothes, and asked him to pick some betel-nuts for her. When he came out of the house, his soldiers took him for her husband and killed him, so that Pingkan's honour was saved.

Myths try to convey something to us—through in a different form than history. Kartini the myth and Kartini the historical person are two very different things, but basically the message is the same.

Mary, the fully liberated human being
The importance of raising woman's awareness of her self-worth cannot be over-emphasized. Always accepting that God transcends all human understanding, we could make use here of the significance of the feminine aspects of divinity—which will be done at length in the chapter on theological motifs—and also of the real meaning of the

symbol of Mary, in order to restore woman's true image of herself.

Protestantism, especially the Calvinist variety, has not displayed much interest in Mary. Except for children's pageants at Christmas and Easter, Mary is invisible in the Reformed churches. The Lutherans and Anglicans do a little better, with their pictures and statues and special days for Mary.

Many feminists, including feminist theologians, have rejected the model of Mary. This is quite understandable when one looks at the standard portrayal of Mary, made first to fit feudalism, then capitalism.

Statues or paintings usually depict her as sugar-sweet, fragile, with eyes either modestly downcast or upturned to heaven—not quite here-and-now! Such a presentation of Mary is, of course, an extremely useful means of domesticating women and other oppressed people. After all, didn't Mary say: "I am the Lord's servant, may it happen to me as you have said"?

Women—and other deprived groups—were supposed to be imitators of Mary, whose sanctity was said to be the result of such submissive "feminine" docility that it invited the highest graces from God the Creator. As Tissa Balasuriya points out, God, of course, was always represented as a man, and an old man at that.

Firstly, it is strange that the privilege of imitating Mary was reserved exclusively to certain people only. Secondly, submission to *God* is something different altogether from submission to human beings.

Mary's submission to the will of God is in no way the abject submission of a slave who has no choice. On the contrary, it is the creative submission of the fully liberated human being, who—not being subject to any other human being—is free to serve God. It is the submission of Abraham, of Moses, leaving the safety of familiar structures to embark on a journey into the unknown.

To many of us, reading or hearing the story of Mary is like reading or hearing a story of which we already know the ending. We know that Joseph is not going to abandon her, and that he is not going to throw her to the wolves. The penalty for a betrothed virgin being with child by a third party was, after all, death. We know everything is "going to be all right".

Therefore, there is not sufficient awe in us at the incredible courage of this young woman, who said what she said: "May it happen to me as you have said."

Often, the church has the unfortunate tendency to concentrate on the trivial, and entirely overlook the essential principle.

Why is Mary considered worthy of veneration?

On account of her virginity? Mary is presented as the ideal of womanhood, in no way "tarnished" by sexual relations. In the litany that honours her, she is invoked in the Roman Catholic Church as "Virgin Most Chaste, Virgin Most Pure, Virgin Most Prudent, Virgin Most Faithful" and only twice referred to as Mother: "Mother Most Pure, Mother Inviolate." Her physical virginity has been greatly emphasized and extolled.

This naturally raises the question what the deepest meaning of virginity really is. The virgin goddesses, the moon goddesses of the ancient religions could by no means be seen as physical virgins, abstaining from and repelling any sexual contact.

In all ages and places people have conceived of a Great Mother, a Goddess watching over humankind from the sky or from the place of the gods. This Great Mother—called *Magna Mater* in Latin—has certain clearly defined qualities: she is Goddess of the Moon, partaking of the characteristics of the moon, and being in a peculiar sense the woman's deity. She was worshipped in ancient Babylonia, in medieval Europe (where she is worshipped to this day among the peasants), in both Americas, in Africa, India, ancient China, Australasia and Polynesia. She always has a son, almost invariably by virgin birth.[3]

It might seem a little strange to think of Mary as related to the ancient moon goddesses, but there is ample evidence to show that she might have been their direct descendant.

Orthodox Catholic fathers call Mary "The Moon of the Church", "Our Moon", "The Spiritual Moon", "The Perfect and Eternal Moon". Pope Innocent III exhorted the sinner to look towards the moon "still in the horizon: Mary,

under whose influence thousands every day find their way to God". In Catholic European countries peasants constantly make this identification. In France, the moon is called *Notre Dame*—"Our Lady" (consider how many great churches in Europe are consecrated to Our *Lady*!); while in Portugal the moon is called "the mother of God".

The Great Mother was always represented as "virgin", a term which needs some investigation as it obviously lacked the modern connotation of "chaste" and "innocent". The Babylonian Ishtar was referred to both as the "Holy Virgin" and the "Prostitute". The Greek Artemis, also Virgin, was goddess of fecundity but not of wedlock.[4]

Virgin meant no more than an unmarried woman: a woman who was her own mistress. It may be used of a woman who has had much sexual experience, it may even be applied to a prostitute. The temple prostitutes were called "the holy virgins". In Greek, children born out of wedlock were called *parthenioi*, "virgin born". And the correct Latin expression for the untouched virgin is not *virgo*, but *virgo intacta*.

If we recognize religious concepts as symbolic, we realize that the term "virginity" must refer to a quality, an inner attitude, not to a physiological or external fact. When used of the Virgin Mary or of the virgin goddesses of other religions, it cannot denote a factual situation, for the quality of virginity persists in spite of sexual experience, childbearing and increasing age.

Protestants do not subscribe to the belief that Mary was ever Virgin, as it is recognized by tradition that she bore carnal children to Joseph, who are referred to in the Gospel as "the brothers and sisters of the Lord".

It is interesting to see how, at certain heights of Catholic speculation, Mary's excellence was made to derive from her divine *motherhood*, while Catholic spirituality tended to define her greatness primarily in terms of her *virginity*.[5]

The Council of Ephesus in A.D. 451 was a council of the undivided Church in which Orthodox, Roman and Reformed have their common roots. In this Council, Mary was proclaimed *Theotokos*, "Mother of God".

Some Protestants may be surprised to rediscover this. So may some Catholics. And it should not be overlooked that, although the faithful may have sung hymns for centuries to the Theotokos, they still insisted that woman lift up her heart through *man*, thus reducing her to a purely biological person.

Giving life for God

To return to the question asked earlier: *Why* was Mary considered worthy of veneration in the first place?

On account of her virginity as understood in its primal sense: that of the liberated human being, who—not being subject to any other human being—is free to serve God. The image seeks to convey that God takes the initiative and the human being is receptive.

This is the deepest meaning of virginity. As Catharina Halkes put it so beautifully, it is a positive stance, rather than a negative dis-stance (in German it is actually *Haltung*, "attitude", and *Ent-haltung*, "abstinence").

In woman's theology, "virgin" can be the symbol for the autonomy of woman. Virgin, then, would not primarily mean a woman who abstains from sexual intercourse (a construction put on it later), but a woman who does not lead a "derived" life (as "daughter/wife/mother" of): a woman who matures to wholeness within herself as a complete person, and who is open for others. Through this maturing process, she is *fertile*, she *gives life* for God.

Not only Virgin, but also Mother. These concepts attain a new power of imagery which may liberate woman from the previous concept of virgin mother—a biological impossibility!—which was being held up to her as a model. In its own way, this previous concept of virgin mother was just as unacceptable as the other model for woman, namely that of Eve the *temptress*. In the Christian milieu it has been commonly recognized that woman escapes being evil (Eve the temptress) only by becoming super-holy (Mary the Virgin Mother). As very few women manage that Great Leap, they are always evil.

It is not at all my intention to depreciate physiological virginity, or for that matter chastity and celibacy. But I do object when it is turned into a cult, as is often the case, and especially when it becomes an encretism* for women only.

Virginity is a noble thing when related to a worthy purpose. There are wise virgins and foolish virgins. Some may be virgins to pave the way to a convenient bachelor- or spinster-hood. To others, it might be the reverse: their virginity liberates them to a dangerous mission, out of love and commitment to others.

Celibacy, as an effort to emulate the absolute poverty and obedience of Christ,[6] is a great sign. Outside of this context of evangelical poverty, however, it is an empty sign. "Virgin Most Pure" is meaningful chiefly when it is also "Virgin Most Poor". (I will elaborate on the concept of evangelical poverty in the chapter on socio-political realities.)

The vow of chastity should not be seen as a status symbol, as at least one eminent Asian Catholic theologian, Father Aloysius Pieris (himself a celibate), has said. Celibacy and marriage do not represent two degrees of holiness, but two different accentuations of the Church's bridal sanctity.[7]

Mary: a wider context

It is no coincidence that lately more importance is being given to Mary, both in Catholic dogma and in Protestant thinking.

Asian Catholics, for example, are beginning to see her no longer as the "fairy queen oozing out sweet piety", but rather as "the mature and committed (Asian) woman, the peasant mother who cheerfully wears herself out to feed and clothe her carpenter son; the worker's wife wearing holy furrows on her face... an image reflected in millions of Asian village mothers today".

Protestants, if they have learned to overcome their initial fear of "mariolatry", might find their sign of hope in her as

---

*Encretism (from *encreteia*, Greek for celibacy): celibacy cult. It made its presence felt in the first milennium when pressure was exerted on Church authorities to pass a law restricting priesthood to celibates, which was resisted by the papacy who feared that any law of compulsory celibacy would give legal sanctions to the encretistic learnings prevalent in the Church at the time.

the first fully liberated human being, whose Magnificat is central in the theology of liberation.

Protestant thinking definitely has a blind spot where Mary is concerned. In the Federal Republic of Germany, a woman theologian drew up a list of instances in the Bible concerning "Jesus and women", to be studied by a women's group. Looking over the list, I asked the group whether they had noticed a significant omission. Nobody had—and everyone was much surprised when I pointed out that there was not a single reference to Mary, who was after all, the first, and perhaps the most important, woman in Jesus' life!

There is a cartoon by Joe Noonan on the wall of the World Council of Churches' editorial office in Geneva which provides food for thought. It depicts Joseph and Mary. She is obviously pregnant, and wears a halo round her head. Joseph—a young man, not the superannuated version which became so popular after the third century (to account for Mary's perpetual virginity, no doubt)—asks her: "When you're the Mother of God, will you still be my Mary?" The caption reads: "Do we ever think that they loved each other? 'Joseph my husband'—'Mary my wife.' A child listens. And grows. And becomes the lover of humankind."

Jesus did not grow up in a vacuum. What strength did the man Jesus draw from the woman of the Magnificat? What gentleness?

Thinking of Mary, I do not exult in her supposed purity, for that is too narrow a perspective which does her no justice. I see her in the wider context of love and self-giving. I admire and appreciate her sensitivity to social injustices and her readiness to take moral risks for the sake of a needed social change.

That is on one level. On another level, I see Mary as the pre-eminent model of humanity, growing into the full image of God. As the receptive Virgin (receptive to the action of God) and the creative Mother (sharing the mission of bringing the good news of salvation to the world), she is the model not only for woman, but also for man. She is the new human being (man-woman), receptive before God, who calls him/her to be *imago Dei*.

Human liberation often seems to be a grim and joyless struggle. The Magnificat shows otherwise. And I exult in the fact that this Asian woman, this Mary, upon her encounter with God bursts out into this great song of thanksgiving and joy given to God, who liberates through the oppressed themselves. Through Mary, women in some special way personify the oppressed, although she represents all oppressed peoples, not just women.

Mary is the truly liberated, fully liberated human being: compassionate and free.

III. Socio-political realities

Exploitation of non-persons

Most people in Asia are exploited, have been exploited, and perhaps cannot conceive of a future in which they will not be exploited. They have to fight for their very existence—to say nothing of social justice and human dignity.

Take a look at the chart overleaf, depicting the socio-economic structure of Sri Lanka. It could be applied to many other Asian countries: 3.5% dominate 96.5%; 15.7% with some luck also get a chance at dominating 80.8%—who never had a choice to begin with.

Women, already exploited on account of their sex, also bear their share of the oppression indicated in this chart. They are more vulnerable to harassment in employment and to violence, they have less access to education, they have no adequate political representation, and so on.

When one has been conditioned to think of categories or groups of people as "non-persons", one sub-consciously sees them as objects to be used or disposed of at will.

Imperialism, racism, sexism, expressed in exploitation, are all aspects of the same attitude, which denies the Other (i.e. the non-person, the object) the right to exist.

The rape of women, of races, of nations, of human and natural resources is justified as serving the mode of—whose?—existence. Women become objects rather than subjects, as Asian airline advertisements illustrate so dramatically (see Appendix III).

The impact of colonialism on the Third World should never be underestimated. How many Europeans—and many good church people—look at the overwhelming poverty of Asia and say self-righteously: "We should never have left in the first place. Things were different when we were still in control!" They have never even tried to assess the way natural economy was destroyed by colonialist policy. Would so many Indonesians be so poor today if the Dutch colonialist government had refrained from their *Cultuur-stelsel*, which forced the peasants to grow products for the European market instead of for their own nurture? What about Bangla Desh and the monolithic jute culture?

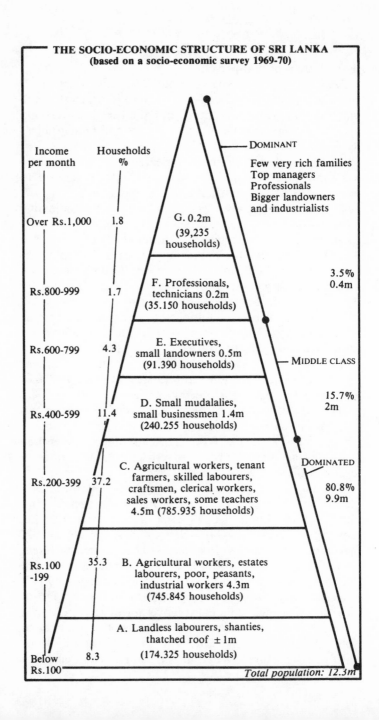

THE SOCIO-ECONOMIC STRUCTURE OF SRI LANKA
(based on a socio-economic survey 1969-70)

Income per month	Households %		
		DOMINANT	
		Few very rich families Top managers Professionals Bigger landowners and industrialists	
Over Rs.1,000	1.8	G. 0.2m (39,235 households)	
Rs.800-999	1.7	F. Professionals, technicians 0.2m (35.150 households)	3.5% 0.4m
Rs.600-799	4.3	E. Executives, small landowners 0.5m (91.390 households)	MIDDLE CLASS
Rs.400-599	11.4	D. Small mudalalies, small businessmen 1.4m (240.255 households)	15.7% 2m
Rs.200-399	37.2	C. Agricultural workers, tenant farmers, skilled labourers, craftsmen, clerical workers, sales workers, some teachers 4.5m (785.935 households)	DOMINATED 80.8% 9.9m
Rs.100 -199	35.3	B. Agricultural workers, estates labourers, poor, peasants, industrial workers 4.3m (745.845 households)	
Below Rs.100	8.3	A. Landless labourers, shanties, thatched roof ± 1m (174.325 households)	

Total population: 12.3m

**THE DISTRIBUTION OF HOUSEHOLDS AND TOTAL INCOME
BY INCOME GROUPS IN Rs. '000**

INCOME GROUPS	WHOLE ISLAND: No. OF HOUSEHOLDS	%	TOTAL INCOME	%	AVERAGE MONTHLY INCOME Rs
A. Below 100	174,325	8.3	13,135.5	2.2	75
B. 100-199	745,845	35.3	111,235.3	18.2	151
C. 200-399	785,935	37.2	218,124.9	35.7	278
D. 400-599	240,255	11.4	114,950.5	18.8	478
E. 600-799	91,390	4.3	62,596.3	10.2	685
F. 800-999	35,150	1.7	31,540.2	5.2	897
G. 1000 +	39,235	1.8	58,988.4	9.7	1,503
Total	2,112,135	100.0	610,571.0	100.0	289

Even today "conquest" is the watchword in Asia. The film *Who Owns the Sky?* is a poignant description of what has happened to Japan, the country poets described a thousand years ago as *mizuho no kuni Yamato*—the blessed isles of Yamato (Great Peace): a country of crystal-clear waters, blue skies and rolling rice-fields.

The waters are not so clear any more, and the air is so polluted that people literally die of it. Because of protests from the townspeople of Chiba, the Kawasaki steel company obligingly moved its plant to the Philippines.

Obviously, the fate of Japan is due to a false concept of development, rooted in the attitude of conquest. The Anti-God, who lives on human sacrifice, has instilled these false concepts.

There is a beautiful beach in Bali from which you can watch glorious sunsets. Until a dozen or so years ago, the local people mainly earned their living through fishing, and the beach was lined with fishing boats. Now that hotel syndicates have discovered just how lucrative beautiful beaches and glorious sunsets can be, you will not see a single fishing boat. Now people earn their living by providing accommodation to young tourists willing to rough it, and by catering to the older variety who want to eat fresh lobster in comfort.

Prostitution, male and female, has soared. In other words, from the productive sector, people have switched almost entirely to the service sector.

The well-known Indonesian writer Anak Agung Pandji Tisna, a Balinese prince who grew up in pre-war Bali—which was closed to all but a select handful of foreigners—once said to me: "When I was young, I really believed that we had much to learn from these westerners. They knew so much we didn't know. They were so refreshingly free from the age-old court inhibitions which restricted my life, and their independence stimulated me.

"Now, when I take a look at these unwashed, uncouth youngsters, those miserable apologies for human beings that infest our beaches, I ask myself: Is this development?"

I have also asked myself this question many times. In the Federal Republic of Germany—an affluent country with one of the world's highest Gross National Products—I visited a car factory. I looked with awe at the assembly-lines, staffed by women and men of whom half were foreigners *(Gastarbeiter)*. There were signs everywhere urging the people to work even harder, of course without affecting the quality of the product. That day's output was 109% already—but apparently that was not enough. In some places the heat and the air were unbearable, even for a few minutes. I felt the spray was getting into my eyes, my lungs. The foreman, seeing my face, remarked: "Ja, sehen Sie, liebe Frau, wenn man keine reiche Eltern hat, dann kommt man hier!" ("Well, you see, madam, if you don't have rich parents, this is where you end up!")

Mammon: the Enemy within

What is development? Is it only to be measured in terms of productivity quotas and the literacy statistics? Is it being concerned for the welfare of *all*—or aiming at higher GNPs and thus ensuring the wealth of a few?

Instead of serious planning for community health, we tend to go for expensive, ineffective, modern hospitals. Instead of "leading people to the gate of wisdom", our education further enslaves them through the pursuit of certificates and degrees.

Where is Christ in this craze for development?

In doing Asian theology, we cannot limit ourselves to beautifully worded abstract concepts. Of course well-fed, well-dressed bourgeois theologians have all the time in the world for that. But if one really encounters the powerless Christ in the oppressive structures of Asia (and indeed everywhere), it's very clear that time is running out.

The face of the exploited non-person is the face of Christ. The abject poverty in which most Asians live (except for the 2.5 or 3.5% who dominate the rest) is the poverty of Christ.

Freedom from poverty is worth striving for, but only if it is tempered by the freedom that comes from poverty.[1] In the first instance, poverty is inflicted poverty; in the second, it is the religious understanding of poverty, or evangelical poverty, i.e. the absence of acquisitiveness or avarice.

In our present stage of development, the Asian society must realize that the primary concern is not the eradication of (inflicted) poverty, but the struggle against Mammon, who is the real poverty-maker. It is not because Asia is "so poor" that people suffer. Indonesia, for example, was estimated by a World Bank Survey last year to be the second richest country in the world in natural resources.

There is plenty to go around, but Mammon grabs most of it; Mammon being "that undefinable force which organizes itself within every person and among persons to make material wealth anti-human, anti-religious, and oppressive".

Mammon is not merely an Enemy outside, he is also the Enemy within. Mammon is every person's innate tendency to use the Other for his/her advantage.

If Christians learned to live in evangelical poverty, if they really worshipped the living God instead of Mammon—or the Anti-God—there would be less poverty inflicted in the world.

In this light, perhaps we can take a more critical view of the massive development programmes by which Asian churches tend to consolidate themselves into big private educational, technological or agricultural establishments run with foreign aid. Do they really serve their aim, do they really alleviate the suffering of the masses? Or do they merely inculcate certain values in certain people, who come to think that a middle-class life-style is the sign of the Kingdom?

Freedom from poverty may then turn into an enslaving pursuit ending in hedonism. Gratify each and every desire, and you've got your reason for living.

Asian Christians should look towards the other major religions of Asia, whose thrust is to teach their followers the way to interior liberation and purification from self-seeking and exploitative instincts.

Asian theology includes two dimensions of liberation: that of society, and that of the person.

In this liberation process, no doubt "the comfortable will be disturbed, as the disturbed will be comforted", to quote Tissa Balasuriya. This is the challenge to the Asian Christian; more especially, to the Asian Christian woman. For often, she is "better off" than her sisters who—in terms of overall exploitation—are doubly exploited. In a context of nation-wide oppression, they are doubly oppressed.

There is a new type of woman emerging in Asia: cosmopolitan, well-educated, well-situated. Not so bound by domestic chores as her sisters in the West, often hers could be the voice that speaks out "for the voiceless", for her oppressed sisters. This is an option which can come only from identification with her sisters, not merely intellectually, but by a life experience: being with and joining in the struggle of the oppressed. Constantly and consistently saying "no" to Mammon, the Anti-God that is evident in the socio-political realities crippling Asia today.

The position of women

When writing about a theme as vast as "women in Asia", one is bound to generalize. It is also quite possible that one applies certain categories, perhaps acceptable in the West with its fairly long history of transition from agricultural to industrial society, which are not immediately relevant to Asia.

I object to Asian societies being called "backward", apparently because they are being compared to the affluence of industrialized nations. I have mentioned the example of the car factory. I also note that in western Europe the service sector is staffed mainly by people from southern Europe. Whoever is doing the "dirty work", one can be quite sure he or she will be any nationality but Swiss/West German/Dutch/Swedish. So in view of that sort of exploitation, who is "backward"?

It took western Europe a couple of centuries to reach its present stage, highly developed and perhaps over-industrialized. Although technology originally came from Asia (with the Crusades), Asia on the whole has had less time to absorb the shock of modern technology with all its marvels. For example, neither of my grandmothers left the Minahassa during their lifetime. It was considered a great adventure for my father to go to far-away Amboina in the Moluccas to study at the teacher's college in 1916. Now my siblings and I, engaged in various forms of communication, have to travel extensively, and we feel it is an unexpected boon if our paths happen to cross at Grindelwald, Colombo or Boston. But has our social conscience also developed in proportion with the great leaps made by technology?

In western women's liberation, two important topics of discussion seem to be marriage and the role of women in production.

Perhaps we should take a closer look at the "standard" concepts about marriage. Is it really true that every little girl grew up looking forward to marriage as her main reason for existence, before those militant Women's Libbers started to stir things up?

In medieval Europe only one out of five women attained the blessed state of matrimony. Most of the time war effectively wiped out eligible males. And besides, there was always the aristocracy, never at a loss to think up laws prohibiting marriage in the "lower classes". They were afraid the rabble would increase at too great a rate. First they made it difficult for them to marry, and in the seventeenth century it was actually prohibited for apprentices and servants (men and maids) to get married. If they broke this law, they were punished in the most barbaric fashion; for example, in Bavaria by whipping and imprisonment.[2]

A little earlier in history, things looked rather different. On account of the devastating wars of the Reformation, the population had sunk to as low as a tenth of its original number in many places. Therefore, the church in Franconia decreed at its Nürnberg Assembly in 1650 that "all priests should marry... and every man should be exhorted *from the pulpit* (!) to marry two wives".

Luther, of course, had already given permission to his friend Philipp I, Landgraf (Count) of Hessen, to contract a bigamous marriage. He was supported by Melanchthon and Butzer. After all, Paul had only stipulated that *bishops* should have one wife—he had not said anything about German counts. Luther didn't think bigamy was contrary to Holy Scripture (to which Bebel remarks acidly in a footnote that "anyhow it was in flagrant contradiction with the prevailing moral of the 16th century"), as he wrote to Chancellor Brink in January 1524 with regard to Henry VIII's marriage to Anne Boleyn. However, he found it extremely annoying that Christians should indulge in bigamy, for they ought to know better than that: after all, Christians often had to forego things which were permissible.

And after the Landgraf's marriage in March 1540, Luther wrote imploring him to keep quiet about the whole thing, otherwise the farmers might get ideas, too—and if all and sundry were to follow the count's example, Luther might get more work than he could cope with.

When I was in the German Democratic Republic, I was told the following version of the story: the Landgraf had gone to Palestine on the Crusades. There, a Saracen princess saved his life. This act meant that now she was in mortal danger herself, so the Landgraf took her to Germany with him and obtained dispensation from the Pope (!) to marry her. That's why one can see the tomb of the Landgraf with a wife at each side.

With regard to women in production, before the Reformation it was quite acceptable for women to become Masters (or Mistresses) in a trade. In fact, they were forced into the guilds, so that they would have to observe the same conditions. Women thus worked independently as weavers: linen, wool, tapestry, and so on. They were goldsmiths, bakers, furriers and in many more trades. They were only driven out after the destruction of economy caused by the wars of the Reformation. At first, they were no longer allowed to become Masters of the guilds—with the exception of widows; later, they weren't even accepted as helpers. At the end of the seventeenth century, women were totally excluded from the trades in Germany.

So much for the myth of my childhood, that the Reformation had made an invaluable contribution towards uplifting the status of women and improving the lot of the poor. On a theoretical level it may have intended to; on the practical level we can see that it actually had the adverse effect. We know what the Reformation did for women like Catharina von Bora*—perhaps we should try to think what it did to the farmer's wife whose fields were devastated by conflicting armies, or what it meant to the women weavers, goldsmiths and others, who were pushed out of the guilds and the whole production process.

Women became more and more marginalized, and production became almost exclusively the domain of men. So we end up with the Biedemayer ideal of the housewife, blissfully ignorant of everything but the joys of wifehood and motherhood. Nothing is more lethal to the development of a human being than those middle-class values: men solely engaged in production, women in reproduction. Two opposite poles. The Ideal Man. The Ideal Woman.

Women in Indonesia

Looking at a country like Indonesia, I am inclined to think that the process was slightly different.

As we've seen, Indonesia is a vast, multicultural society structured on traditional patterns. It is also still very much influenced by concepts of cosmic balance, of kinship, common soil and so on. In a society such as this, woman may be subordinated, exploited, oppressed—but she will never be so completely the Other that she has somehow become in the western capitalist technocracies.

---

*Born of an aristocratic family, she entered the convent at age five, and became a nun when adult. Later, she escaped from the convent in a herring-barrel, together with several other nuns. Having refused several other candidates, she eventually proposed to Luther, and became the exemplary German pastor's wife.

She is the partner in production, the co-ancestor of future generations. Without her, there is no cosmic balance. Alienation on the western scale can, therefore, never occur.

Marriage is important, because it not only ensures the procreation of the tribe but it also maintains the cosmic balance. An unmarried man is just as pitiful as an unmarried woman—and just as unacceptable.

Production is, and always has been, a joint affair. Since there has never been a system of the guilds, parents have passed their knowledge and skills on to their children. Some employment opportunities have perhaps been more open to men, others to women. Women are weavers, women are goldsmiths or silversmiths, working together with men. Agriculture always was a joint venture, not in the least because it had mystic connotations.

One should not confuse the situation in which a high-born woman like Kartini found herself, with the daily life realities of the average Javanese woman of her time. That woman would not have had time to go to school, to grow dissatisfied with her life-style. She would be far too busy. She had great freedom of movement and she was quite independent. In 1887 (when Kartini was eight years old) the Dutch missionary Poensen writes: "It is the (Javanese) woman who takes care of the rice, which she has planted, harvested, dried and gleaned. She cooks the rice and the vegetables... she buys the household equipment... she sells the home-grown products... she dyes the cloths which she has woven, and sells them."

Twenty years later Kruiyt, another Dutch missionary, was also impressed by the presence of the Javanese woman in various different spheres: in the market, in the shop, pounding the rice in the village, making batik, brewing herbal medicine, and so on. Woman being such an active factor in the village economy also made her an important member of the community. In this community, each action had been predetermined by tradition, and each member had a special function to fulfil for the good of the whole. To be wife and mother was inseparably connected to this function, and was imperative for the well-being and the continuity of the community.

An aristocratic Javanese woman, on the other hand, did not have to contribute anything to the economic life of the community. Married off at 15 or 16, she lived a very restricted life with little to do except please her husband (who often had scores of concubines to please him, anyway) or look after her children—and she invariably had a retinue of servants to do that, too.

Perhaps a woman like Kartini was oppressed, but she herself was also an oppressor, a fact not taken into account by biographers emoting over the poor little Javanese princess. She proved this conclusively when she agreed to marry the Regent of Rembang, *on condition* that she should be the head wife. Women's liberation in Asia, then, should definitely not model itself after Kartini.

Another thing which should be borne in mind is that the Asian, or rather Indonesian, way of communication is not always analogous to the western. There is a great deal of non-verbal communication.

When I was younger, I was greatly surprised to realize that in our Minahassan languages (the eight tribal languages and the commercial Malay) there was no word for "thank you". The words we used were obviously loan-words from the Dutch and from Malay. Later I discovered that most tribal languages of Indonesia don't have this expression. So also in a few other Asian countries. Does this mean, then, that all these people have no concept of gratitude?

The answer to this is that of course they have such a concept, and the reason there is no verbal expression for it is because they felt that was too limited; they showed their gratitude in other ways. This is something which people who are used mainly to verbal communication may have some difficulty in understanding.

In a patriarchal society like that of the Bataks, for example, it would seem to the casual western observer that the women are terribly oppressed. At the family councils in the north the women have no say at all. In the south, they fare slightly better, but even there it would appear that they are not involved in active decision-making.

In fact, women do have a lot to say, and they do say it. Do they have to say it in the family councils to exercise their power? The message gets through in a slightly different way than in the West, but it gets through.

The relationship between women and men is not just a power relationship between dominated and dominant, oppressed and oppressor. The human factor provides for genuine love and concern, as the following case history may show.

```
CASE STUDY
```

Woman and education

Likas Tarigan comes from Sibolangit, Karoland (North Sumatra). Born in 1924, she finished primary school in 1937, and the school inspector offered her a scholarship to the teachers' college in Padang (Minangkabau, West Sumatra). At the time it was still quite revolutionary for a girl to study, especially if she had to leave the village and the region of her birth.

Likas's mother was very much opposed to the idea. Her father thought it was a good thing. But the person who persuaded her to go was her elder brother.

Likas remembers that he took her for a walk to the outskirts of the village. This in itself was quite extraordinary, for in Karo society, brothers and sisters were not encouraged to communicate with each other after having reached the age of puberty, except when strictly necessary.

On the road leading out of the village several people passed on their way to the market. Presently a family came by: the man walked in front, without a care in the world. The woman staggered under the weight of the heavy burden on her head: parcels containing foodstuffs and household utensils. Furthermore, two children were clinging to her sarong, a third one at her breast.

"Look at that woman," said her brother. "Do you want to be like her when you grow up? I do not want my sister's future to be such."

Likas recalls that her brother's love and genuine concern for her, and moreover his belief in her ability to shape a better future, were the driving factors in her life. She was the first girl to leave her village. Her mother wept and wailed, claiming Likas's departure would be the death of her. Her brother supported her financially from his salary as policeman (he was in the vice squad, combating prostitution and the import of women from Hong Kong and other places). But both her mother and brother died before she finished school, to her great sorrow.

She was assigned to a girls' school in Pangkalan Brandan. Her father, who had remarried, sent his little son to live with her. When the war (the Second World War) reached Indonesia, her father braved artillery fire and bombings to get "his child" home to the comparative safety of the village. Likas was quite hurt to realize that, being "only a daughter", her father's concern didn't include her.

At the time there was a group of young Karo men and women in Medan, who met periodically for discussions. One evening Likas was asked to speak on the position of women in Karo society. She deplored the conditions in which a Karo woman had to live: with a full load of work in the house and in the field, the woman was responsible for the family and the income, while the husband spent his time in the local coffee-shop playing chess and drinking with the other men.

The young men present did not take kindly to this evaluation of Karo life-style. One of them, Jamin Gintings, engaged her in a spirited discussion. He followed her home, trying to show her the flaws of her way of reasoning, but she refused to take back a single word. The next meetings of the young Karo people became a public debating ground for the two antagonists.

In due course, they decided to get married—which was also unheard of at the time, because marriages were usually arranged by the families. Personal preference was negligible. However, Likas's father gave his consent, and she married the young man who was later to become an outstanding leader in Indonesian society: an army general, and eventually, ambassador to Canada.

After her marriage, Likas found her husband to be a great source of support in her involvement with women's liberation.

During the Karo Culture Seminar in 1958, Likas tried to propose a change of the inheritance laws. In Karo patriarchal society, daughters don't inherit anything. This is a gross injustice, because in actual fact it is the daughters who work very hard to supplement the family income. Unfortunately, the proposal was rejected.

Jamin Gintings himself always tried to conscientize the Karo people with regard to their women. It is a tradition in Karo society that the guest of honour is presented with special food when visiting the villages. After Jamin Gintings had won renown as a great leader, this always happened at feasts given for him. The chiefs would present him with a platter of the most choice food, shouting: "This platter we present to the honoured son of our country, the great general Jamin Gintings, whom we respect above all others!"

Jamin Gintings, after accepting the plate, invariably passed it on to his wife, shouting: "And I pass on this plate to my honoured wife, whom I respect above all others!"

In this way he tried to raise the awareness of the Karo people to the invaluable and indispensable contribution of the women in the life of the society.

After the death of her husband a few years ago, Likas herself became politically active. She was a candidate of the Golongan Karya (task force, i.e. the government party) in North Sumatra. This is especially interesting in view of the fact that one of the major objections raised against the ordination of women in the Karo church was the assertion that "it is unseemly in Karo culture for a woman to give her opinion or to be involved in the decision-making process".

* * * * *

The political participation of women

In the struggle for Indonesian independence, women were as active as men. In fact, a great Indonesian statesman said in 1939: "The women's movement was born in the twentieth century as a full sibling *(adik kandung)* of the Indonesian nationalist movement." (Adinegoro: "Soal Ibu", *Keutamaan Istri* 21 April 1939.)

All over Indonesia, women's movements or organizations had come into being. Political parties and youth groups had their women's section. From the youth organizations eventually Indonesia Muda, Young Indonesia, was born, in which women were accepted as full members.

In the above-mentioned women's youth organizations, two significant changes occurred: firstly, in the general attitude of men towards women. Men came to realize that women were good comrades-in-arms, and possessed equal capabilities, rights and responsibilities. Secondly, young people of such different ethnic backgrounds started to become aware of themselves as *Indonesians*, rather than Young Javanese, Young Sumatrans, Young Amboinese and so on. In other words, they overcame both their male chauvinist and their regional chauvinist attitudes. This was reflected in the Sumpah Pemuda ("oath of the youth") of 1928, which said: "We the sons and daughters of Indonesia vow to have one motherland... one nation... one language—Indonesia." *

The burning issues for women at that time were: education—more specifically co-education—and marriage, which covered polygamy (polygyny), child marriage, and the status of women in marriage, more especially, their lack of say in the matter.

In the *Volksraad* (people's council) of the colonial government which was founded in 1918, there were continuing discussions with regard to the appointment of women. The colonial minister Pleyte felt it was only fitting to appoint women to the council, as this was in accordance with the *adat*, which had always given women a say in family councils.

When the government refused, an eminent Minahassan, A.L. Waworuntu, Regent of Sonder, declared in the council: "With this act the legislator has effectively wiped out an ancient and honoured custom of the Minahassans. According to the old *adat*, women have the same rights as men, not only in their immediate families, but also in the clans."

---

*The word *tumpah darah*, which I have translated as "motherland", literally means "blood shed", obviously referring to the process of childbirth.

An organization worth mentioning is the P4A: Perkumpulan Pembasmian Perdagangan Perempuan dan Anak, founded in 1930. Its aim was, as its name says, "to eradicate the traffic of women and children". Its members were women and men, who among other things petitioned the government in 1940 to increase its number of officers in the vice squad, and to appoint women there also. They also urged immigration officials to be more thorough, and customs officials to be more critical in the import of films or printed matter. Women should also be on the censor board.

I have often regretted that this particular organization seems to have disappeared without a trace, as its concerns seem to be more urgent than ever nowadays. Of course, people take a more sophisticated view of the traffic in women and children now than they did in those unenlightened days before GNP.

It must be admitted that the women's movements mentioned above only affected certain strata of the society—a very small percentage indeed. Actually, things did not change very much for the other women: the peasant, the labourer and the plantation worker.

The Indonesian Republic declared its Independence on 17 August 1945, shortly after Japan surrendered.

In paragraph 27 of the constitution, it is stated that *all citizens are equal before the law*, and that each citizen is entitled to employment and living in accordance with human dignity.

Hence, from its very inception, the Indonesian Republic has recognized that the position of women is equal to that of men. In the first cabinet, a woman, Maria Ulfah Santoso, served as Minister of Social Welfare, later becoming cabinet secretary. Another woman, S.K. Trimurti, was Minister of Labour for eleven years.

In the present cabinet, there are only two women, both of them junior ministers. One of them is in charge of women's participation. Such, then, is the great achievement of the women's movements—women even have their very own minister!

In 1950, nine women became members of the Provisory People's Congress, which had a total membership of 225. In

1955, 18 women were appointed to the first parliament (271 members). In 1977, 33 out of 460 MPs were women.

Women have risen to the ranks of ambassadors, judges, prosecutors, attorneys, chiefs of bureaux, and other important positions. On this level, there is no discrimination, and they receive pay equal with men. The blatant exploitation of women occurs on a different level.

Women in the rural areas

In Indonesia, the working woman's life is essentially rural, as 85% of the population live in villages. Nearly 95% of the female work force is engaged in agriculture, or in industries such as textile-making, batik, and foodstuffs.

The greatest problem in rural areas is the absence of adequate sanitation facilities as an effective measure to ensure community health. People often live at subsistence levels. Statistics show that 85% of all female children under five in Indonesia are undernourished.

Seen in the overall context of poverty, this may not be surprising. There are entire villages where children are cretins because of malnutrition. However, the malnourishment of female children may be attributed to the fact that they are often the ones who get the least food; fathers and brothers get first priority.

It would be far wiser to inculcate good eating habits and a responsible sharing of food, and introduce adequate sanitation facilities—such as the provision of fresh water—rather than aim at expensively equipped hospitals.

It has already been pointed out that throughout Asia, ordinarily the power is held by a very small section of the population, "the upper class", who are also the most articulate and literate. The people as a whole remain inarticulate, passive, unorganized to defend their interests.

Who, then, does the Church identify with? Is she really only interested in "being a guest at the rich people's table", instead of trying to serve the poor?

To make it worse, the Church in Indonesia often presents a false concept of ministry through holding lavish Christmas dinners, elaborate fêtes, and other such events.

The nutrition situation in the underdeveloped countries has generally not improved since before World War II; in many countries, it might even have deteriorated. The FAO has pointed out that the majority of people in such countries suffer to some degree from undernutrition or malnutrition. In South Asia, people spent two-thirds or more of their income on food.

Of course it must be said that the church does carry out development programmes. National Councils of Churches have their development centres, which are very much concerned with the issues mentioned above. However, there does not seem to be any relation between the worship service (with lavish dinners and fêtes) and the institutionalized Christian witness of the development programmes. It might seem a bit schizophrenic, perhaps even hypocritical, for the church to have both at the same time.

What has to be worked out is how best to serve the rural poor. They may live at subsistence level, but they are still comparatively better off than those who migrate to the big cities, thus swelling the number of the urban poor.

It is difficult even for healthy children to have a reasonable chance of survival in society. How much more so for the handicapped!

```
CASE STUDY
```

A handicapped child

Early in 1977, a woman gave birth to her sixth child, a son, in the village of Watublapi, Flores (Eastern Lesser Sunda Islands). The child appeared to be in good health, except for the fact that his legs were mere stumps: the left one ended slightly below the knee-cap, while the right one was slightly longer. Also, on his right arm, just above the wrist, an indentation ran all round it.

The mother was so ashamed at having produced such an imperfect child that she hid him in the house for nearly a year. Although she fed him and took good care of him, she never took him outdoors.

Then a Belgian social worker stationed with the Catholic mission of the area learned of the child's existence. She visited the mother and persuaded her to show her the child.

"Why, what a lovely boy," Sister Marie-Jeanne said. "He looks bright, too. Why don't you take him out, so he can have some sunshine and fresh air?"

Eventually, the mother overcame her reluctance to show the child to others, and even allowed him to be taken to the Catholic mission, where he was able to get some elementary medical attention.

Through the mission, the child was eventually sent to Jakarta, to have prostheses fitted and also to undergo some surgery on his arm. If the constricted blood vessels were not widened, his hand would fail to get an adequate blood supply, and remain infant size all his life.

Franciscus, as he was called, learned to walk very quickly. He also proved to be very alert and intelligent for his age.

The problem is that he will have to change prostheses every other year, to keep pace with his growth. So far, private persons have been financing him, and the doctors have operated free of charge. A West German supplier of orthopedic appliances is also willing to provide the prostheses free of charge. However, this situation is not sustainable for an extended period.

* * * * *

Living by the law

In the rural areas, people still live very much by the *adat*.

Adat is the tradition, customs and culture of each tribe or ethnic group. With so many different ethnic groups and/or tribes, Indonesia has a complex set of laws, which also include the *adat* law (customary law).

Originally, this *adat* law was intended to maintain cosmic balance, thus preserving the tribe from all evil. As long as one observed the proper rites, and lived in the prescribed way of the ancestors, one—and thus the tribe—would be safe.

In such a traditional society, it is the tribe, not the person, who is important. Marriage is entered into for the preservation of the tribe, not for the personal gratification of those concerned.

In this context, it may be easier to understand why dowry is so important. Dowry here means bride-price, as opposed to the custom in India and Sri Lanka, where it is the bride's family which has to pay.

It is understandable that in the United Nations' Declaration against the Discrimination of Women (1967), dowry is specially named as being one of the "forms of slavery" to be combated. In Indonesia, the church has usually taken a strong stand against it, so much so that in the Minahassa (where dowry has been prohibited since the nineteenth century) it has disappeared from tradition completely.

The attempts of several Indonesian churches today (e.g. the Nias Church) to abolish dowry through severe application of church discipline—for example, people who practise giving/accepting dowry are refused Holy Communion—are understandable, but in my opinion not quite the right approach to ministry. The abolition of dowry should not just be imposed from "up above". It would be far better to work from the grassroot level, instilling the concept of personhood.

It is not so much the monetary value of dowry which is important, but rather the mystic value. If the tribe is seen to consist of different clans (the usual system is that there are three main clans: the ego-clan, the bride-givers, and the bride-acceptors), moving a person from one clan to the other seriously disrupts the cosmic balance. Hence, payment has to be made in the form of articles with a high mystic content (in some tribes, for example, human heads were an indispensable part of the dowry) to try to restore the balance. Although people have been liberated on a rational level of belief in the mystic content of dowry, on an emotional level they still attach great importance to it.

In most traditional societies, the clan of the bride-givers (i.e. the clan of one's mother) is held in very high esteem. The Karo Bataks call this clan *Dibata si idah*, "the visible God". On no account should this clan be offended. At traditional feasts, they get the seats of honour, and are served the best part of the meat. To offend the relatives on the father's side is bad enough as it is, but to offend the mother's side of the family is quite unpardonable.

It is interesting to see that in the tribal languages there are no words, no concept, for the high God. The word used for God is usually the same as that for ancestor, for example: *Ompung* in Batak, *Opo'* in Minahassa.

In other matters relating to *adat*, the Indonesian churches sometimes fail to take a clear stand. For example, ecumenism is preached all over Indonesia, but pastors who take spouses from other tribes (something which is becoming increasingly common, thanks to the co-educational system of Indonesian theological seminaries) often face great problems when they return to their own cultural context. Usually, the wife follows the husband—in which case the bride-givers often feel they have been slighted. The church may make soothing noises, but is itself not always grateful for having acquired an extra pastor without cost.

The people often do not perceive how the *adat*, originally conceived of to preserve the community from evil, has in itself become evil. Instead of protecting people, it oppresses them. It has become a manifestation of the *stoicheia tou kosmou* (Galatians 4), just like the Anti-God is a manifestation of Mammon.

Women in the urban areas

Many young women of the urban areas are lured to the big cities with promises of work in the factories or as domestic servants. Once they arrive, they are then forced into prostitution. In Indonesia, although prostitution is theoretically a legal offence, it is condoned. When not legalized, it is localized.

I find it interesting that in the tribal societies, prostitution is not known. It came with increased mobility and commercialization. Doesn't this indicate the degree of alienation a person has to experience to start treating sex, the most intensive of human relationships, as a commodity? (If the sexual union somehow reflects the hypostatic union of the Godhead, as some theologians have claimed, should it be so demeaned?)

Bebel claims: "Prostitution is an indispensable institution for the bourgeois society, just like the police, the army, the church and enterprise."

Prostitution is one of the burning issues in Asia today. As pointed out above, there is a very real link between tourism and prostitution. It is also linked to the presence of foreign military bases and transnational companies.[3]

Where tourism has become an integral part of the country's economic programme, one should not be too surprised if there is no great enthusiasm to search for viable alternative occupations for the prostitutes.

The Church does not exhibit an attitude of love and acceptance to the prostitutes. More often it is one of judgment and self-righteousness. Recently, a pastor was suspended from service in his church for having had the audacity to marry a prostitute. She was in the so-called high-class bracket, and cynical tongues said that the real reason for the pastor's suspension was the embarrassment felt by some of the church-members to whom she might have been more than just a casual acquaintance.

The double standard is, of course, as old as the Church Fathers. Augustine—who didn't exactly lead a saintly life prior to his conversion—couldn't refrain from crying: "Remove prostitutes from human affairs, and you will unsettle everything because of lust." He was, of course, referring to the *man's* lusts. It was a well-known fact that women, i.e. the respectable ones, didn't have any.

In referring to this passage, Thomas Aquinas, the greatest of Roman Catholic theologians, said: "Prostitution in the cities is like the sewage system in the palace. Do away with it, and the palace will turn into a place of filth and stink." The Provincial Council of 1665 in Milan was of the same opinion.

It is interesting to see how Jesus dealt with prostitutes. Perhaps it is not admissible to say that Mary Magdalene, commonly accepted as the first person Jesus revealed himself to after his Resurrection, was a prostitute. The woman at the well in Samaria (John 4) definitely was, however, yet Jesus treated her as a person, not as an object: a safety-valve for male passion, or part of a sewage system.

An appalling disregard for the dignity of women is also manifested in the Council of Konstanz, 1414-1418. This council is mainly remembered for its indictment of John

Hus, who was burned at the stake for heresy. All church history books record this.

Less attention is given to something else, which is equally revealing to the kind of church renewal the gentlemen of the council had in mind—namely, the fact that the number of prostitutes who came to Konstanz during this time was equal to the number of delegates to the council.

Actually, it must be said that the reputation of the clergy at the time was so bad that the farmers, seeking to protect their wives and daughters from seduction, refused to appoint spiritual counsellors who didn't promise to take concubines, if they didn't have any to start with—a situation which inspired the bishop of Konstanz to levy a special "concubine-tax" from the priests in his diocese.

Consent or exploitation?

The present secular society is one in which practically everything has been transformed into commodities, including human relationships. Sex, as one of the most intensive forms of relationships, has turned into a prime commodity.

In many Asian countries, tourism (hence, prostitution) is one of the most lucrative sectors of the nation's economy. Evidence for this is found in the *Far Eastern Economic Review*, which devoted three whole pages in its 2 March 1979 issue to prostitution in Asia. The article is called "For Singles, Swingers and Others (After Dark)", and is sprinkled with cute remarks which are no doubt intended to show the liberated attitude of the writer. As Enrique Dussel has said: "It is just as bad to say cute things about women as it is to say things against them".

The *Review* is obviously more concerned with economy than with ethics. "*Kisaeng* are traditionally recreational *creatures* (emphasis mine) trained to serve and entertain men," says the article, referring to the swinging life in Korea. "Asia's lights o' love are mostly young, pretty, gay and a welcome change from the hard-faced crones found in the West."

W.S. Rendra, the well-known Indonesian poet, wrote a poignant poem about Maria Zaitun (Mary Olive), a prostitute who was no longer "pretty and gay", though still young, dying of venereal disease on the city garbage-heaps—or, as the *Review* would have put it discreetly, "one of the indispositions Captain Cook's sailors are said to have introduced to the East".

Since then, American GIs have done their share: "Vietnam Rose" is a particularly resistant strain of "one of those indispositions". It became resistant because they could not be bothered to take the whole cure of antibiotics. The GIs have gone home, but the disease lingers on.

An SCM report has estimated that 60% of the women in some areas of Indonesia are prostitutes. Generally, they are driven by economic necessity. Living in conditions of extreme poverty, they are ruthlessly exploited. This is a prime example of the way women tend to bear the burden of double exploitation because of their sex, in an underdeveloped exploited country.

But prostitution exists, the argument goes, with the consent of the prostitutes. Some men claim self-righteously that it is even necessary for the economic survival of the women, so they are really doing a Good Thing—an attitude which is reflected in the above-mentioned article in the *Far Eastern Economic Review*: "In Manila, 'hospitality girls' from one of the small bars... in a gesture of gratitude to some of their favoured clientele, put up a makeshift shrine decorated with the photographs of their top three (journalist) patrons."

As Mary John Mananzan pointed out: "Even when done with the consent of women, the fact that the consent is extracted or even just conditioned by a weakness or position of disadvantage makes the act an act of exploitation."

She goes on to distinguish between the "peaceful" form of sexual exploitation and the violent forms. The former is based on the recognition that the female possesses something of value to the male, which she can be coerced to surrender for a good that appears to her to be, at least for the moment, greater than this value she possesses. The violent forms of sexual exploitation can be traced further back to man's structural capacity for forcible entry into the woman's correspondingly structural vulnerability. In other words: rape, which man comes to see as "a vehicle of his victorious conquest of the woman [being] the ultimate test of his superior strength, the triumph of his manhood".[4]

This possibility of coercion in the exchange of values or the power of intimidation by a superior strength makes sexual exploitation doubly exploitative, and this in third world situations that are compounded by economic, political and social coercion.

Since the 1960's, there has been a remarkable leap in the tourism industry in most Asian countries—take, for example, the Philippines. From being a minor item in the nation's economy, it became the fifth largest dollar-earning industry by the 1970's, according to the statistics on travel and tourism for 1965-1975, published by the statistics division of the Department of Tourism.

In the Philippines, says the *Far Eastern Economic Review*, sex provides a major incentive to the traveller. Whereas in the past Japanese all-male tour groups took night tours in buses which returned to the hotel with double the original number of passengers, a first-class *(sic)* hotel now offers a room package which includes a female companion. For the more discriminating, there are also co-eds, fashion models, movie starlets or teen-age boys.

It should be noted that the women included in the package deals normally get only 15 to 20% of the fee paid by the clients.

Perhaps there are no sufficient indicators to measure the moral degradation that prostitution brings with it. But it is clear that a country that considers tourism as a pillar of its economic development does so at the expense of human dignity, and especially at the cost of the exploitation of its women.

These are the modern human sacrifices, who are devoured daily, not by the tribal gods of old who craved human blood for the sake of cosmic balance but by the Anti-God, by Mammon, for the sake of GNP.

Moral pollution

The presence of foreign military bases is also a factor responsible for prostitution. Angeles and Olongapo in the Philippines are two examples.[5] The dehumanization and corruption, especially among Philippine women, which is brought about by these bases underline the social cost to the country, apart from the military and political implications.

Olongapo, a town of nearly 200,000 people (the home of the Subic Bay Naval Base) is also the working ground of 16,000 prostitutes, of which 10,000 are licenced. There are several thousand illegitimate children of US service-men.

During the Vietnam war, Olongapo had the reputation of being a wide-open area for the GIs R & R (= Rest and Recreation).

This is one aspect of the war which has not been adequately discussed: the social death of a whole community. This is far worse than physical destruction. Wilfully or not, through the Vietnamese war the Americans destroyed what was most precious to the Vietnamese (and, in the same way, to the people of Olongapo, for example), namely: family, friendship, their manner of expressing themselves.[6] From persons, people have turned into objects, commodities, statistics. They become non-persons.

What right does one nation have to make another nation its battleground or its playground? As long as the policies of Asian nations are so determinedly export-oriented and foreign-controlled, this question will continue to be asked.

Yet another factor in the rise of prostitution in Asia is the mushrooming of industrial establishments everywhere, as a result of the incentives to foreign investments.

Aside from ecological pollution, these establishments give rise to moral pollution. In Indonesia, there are the so-called "contract-wives" i.e. the women who live with the contracted foreign workers only for the period of their contracts. An analogue for this may be found in the colonial period, when many Dutchmen kept *nyais* (mistresses) during the period of their stay in the region. Children of such unions were legitimized and sent to Holland, if so lucky—although that almost invariably meant they never saw their mothers any more. Otherwise, when the father declined responsibility, the child often grew up with its mother's relatives, facing all the unpleasantness which is the fate of illegitimate children of such a mixed ancestry even today.

Young girls are employed as maids, laundrywomen, and cooks of the foreign workers. Most of the time they are expected to become their mistresses as well, and very few are in a position to make formal complaints, firstly, because of the fear of being fired, and secondly, because of the inherent shame attached to sexual violation. To these girls, it is literally a fate worse than death. Often, it's the first step towards prostitution, since the girl feels so ashamed and so despised that she thinks nothing much worse can happen to her now.

CASE STUDY

A prostitute

Jakarta Utara (north) is one of the five cities making up the metropolitan district of Greater Jakarta (estimated at six million inhabitants).

Tanjung Priok, the harbour, used to be Indonesia's main gateway to the world, in the days before air travel. It also used to be the area where prostitution flourished most.

Today, prostitution is localized—not legalized—in the area known as Kramat Tunggak. About 3,000 women live in 150 houses, separated from the main street by a high wooden fence. The houses are neatly and conspicuously numbered. About eight women live in each house, together with the madam and her protector. Each woman has her own room, and each house has its sitting room, including a bar. Sanitation facilities are better than average. Generally, there are framed photographs of the women on the wall of the sitting room. The customer points out the woman of his choice, and the madam then gives him the key to her room. The fee is around Rp. 3,000 (US$5,—, new rate), of which the madam takes the lion's share. There are also special "all night" reductions.

Inem is a young girl in her teens. Her father was the pastor in the small East Javanese village where she comes from. A few years ago, the whole family was transmigrated to Kalimantan (Borneo). Inem didn't want to go with them; besides, her brother wanted her to join him in Jakarta, "to get an education".

Inem's parents consented. Her brother kept his promise and sent her to school. He gave her a good home, and she was quite happy to be with him.

One day, he was killed in a traffic accident. His wife, Inem's sister-in-law, said that she couldn't be expected to take responsibility for someone else's offspring. Not only did she turn Inem out of the house, she also contrived to have her become a prostitute.

Inem is now one of the 600 Christian women living in the Kramat Tunggak compound. In Indonesia, one is obliged to state one's religion in the Kartu Penduduk (Civil Registration Card).

Some Ursuline nuns discovered the proportionately high rate of Christians among the inhabitants of the complex. They applied for permission to start a programme which would involve Bible studies, general knowledge and physical education.

Permission was granted, but at first they were not allowed to enter the compound. They had to conduct all their classes in the clerk's office across the road.

The prostitutes are not allowed to leave the compound without permission. Even crossing the road proved to be not without complications. The madams would say: "How do I know you're really going to school with those holy women, and not off to some rendez-vous with a man?" So the women would have to pay their usual commission first, before obtaining permission from the madams.

It wasn't until the Ministry of Social Welfare intervened that the madams stopped harassing the women who attended the classes. Soon, the nuns were also allowed to hold their programme within the compound itself, taking different houses in turn. The attitude of the madams varied. On the whole, they seemed to be willing to cooperate only for fear of rebuke from the ministry.

When we talked with the madam of Inem's house to make enquiries about the possibility of holding the classes there, she was very sociable, insisting that we have some refreshments with her. She kept saying that, although she was not a Christian herself, she had great respect for people who were religious. She never discouraged them from performing their religious duties. For example, it happened to be the month of Ramadhan—the fast of the Muslims—and she did not stop her girls from fasting, although it inevitably affected their work. She said that she always encouraged the girls to broaden their interests, and to get as much education as possible, "so they can serve the country in better ways".

It was not immediately clear in what context she applied the word "better". Apparently, she had been a prostitute herself. This seems to be the only "good" future a prostitute can aspire to: becoming a madam—unless she has the good fortune to get married to a man who does not exploit her. Some prostitutes marry several times: usually, when their savings have gone, so has the man.

"She's such a bright girl, is Ina," said the madam, patting Inem on the back. Apparently she felt Ina sounded more sophisticated than Inem. "I keep telling her to try to get back to school. She's always carrying her Bible with her, reading it whenever she gets the chance."

When we had left the house, we asked Inem, who was allowed to walk us to the gate: "What would you like to do in the future?"

She just smiled.

* * * * *

Rape

In Asia, women are not encouraged to venture out of their homes without male escort after dark. In fact, there are many places where it wouldn't be safe for her to go out alone even before dark.

At the Asian Theological Conference held in Sri Lanka in January 1979, during an informal discussion among the women themselves, somebody asked: "Well, why do you think we're not encouraged to go out after dark?"

"You might be robbed," one suggested.

"Well, men run the same risk of being robbed!"

"You might be robbed *and* raped," someone else said, and that was the general consensus.

From early childhood, the fear of rape is drilled into women, although it is perhaps not always made so obvious.

It is not so long ago that in certain tribal societies of Indonesia, a man had the right to abuse any woman he might happen to find wandering around unprotected in the field or outside the village. The only thing the woman could do in such a case was to try to grab his headkerchief or his dagger, so that she could complain to the man's family later, and through showing the token she had obtained from him, force him to marry her. A wonderful solution, not unlike that of the Book of Leviticus, where the girl also got to marry her rapist, if she was lucky.

Mary Daly has called rape one of the three dimensions of the Most Unholy Trinity.[7] The other two are genocide and war. She mentions the case of the 200,000 Bangla Deshi women, abandoned by their husbands because they had been raped by Pakistani soldiers. (This would probably have gone unnoticed in the world press, which was concentrating on "more important things", had not Kentaro Buma, at the time secretary for the WCC's CICARWS* Asia Desk, called a press conference on the subject.)

Mary Daly cites several other examples of the horrible treatment of the women of Bangla Desh—"women" including "an eight year-old girl, who was found too child-small for the soldiers' purposes (and) slit to accommodate them, and raped until she died."[8]

As Daly points out, all men have their power enhanced by rape, since this instils in women a need for protection. Rape is a way of life.

In the imposition of state control, rape is almost a standard procedure. In the suppression of subversion, prisoners will be tortured. For women prisoners this does not mean just physical violence, but inevitably takes on a sexual tone. Women political detainees are raped: it is the ultimate insult.

In an industrial setting, there are hundreds of cases of women workers sexually exploited by their supervisors and managers. When women do work at home, for example, the supervisors will often refuse to accept their work unless they bring it personally. Promises of better pay, promotion and

*Commission on Inter-Church Aid, Refugee and World Service.

improved working conditions are also standard devices to coerce the woman into accommodating her employer's wishes.

From the examples given above, we see that in the struggle for liberation that is going on throughout Asia, the liberation of women from any form of becoming objects is a necessary facet. There can be no true liberation without it.

We must ask ourselves, over and over again: Is development always to be at the expense of others, of the Other? Do we discover God in this challenge?

Is our struggle motivated by *love*, for the Other, for life? Or are we necrophiliacs, to use Erich Fromm's terminology: in love with dead things—structures, systems, ideologies, commodities, money, computers, etcetera?

Women in urban areas

Jakarta, a sprawling metropolis with around six million inhabitants, is an interesting model for the Asian situation. Slum and skyscraper exist side by side. There are magnificent boulevards in the residential areas, lined with splendid mansions. There are people who are so rich that they have their ice cream especially sent from Manila for their children's birthdays. Then there are people who are so poor that they have no homes of their own, and they make their living mainly from what they find in the garbage cans of the rich.

The bourgeois woman, usually the wife of a civil servant or a successful businessman, does not face some of the problems of her western sisters. Housework is no problem, nor is babysitting, because there are always servants, if one does not live in an extended or joint family.

Perhaps she goes out to work. A great many women work outside the home, as teachers, secretaries, civil servants, and so on. Education is a great asset.

The domestic servants, male or female, usually come from the rural areas, where there are no adequate employment opportunities. They work for room and board and negligible salaries. Their only holidays are at the end of Ramadhan (the Muslim fast), when they go home, bringing presents for their families.

Often they are very young. Although there are labour laws protecting women and minors (for example, women are not allowed to work between 10 p.m. and 6 a.m.), these are rarely observed. The employers often take no interest in the education or spiritual welfare of their servants. They tend to adopt an attitude of: "Well, there are plenty more where you come from," and may dismiss servants over trivial incidents.

Young girls, as already stated above, of course run the extra risk of sexual exploitation. I will conclude this chapter with two case histories, both dealing with "deprived" children.

```
CASE STUDY
```

Deprived child

The Menteng district is the most fashionable residential area in Jakarta. The President lives there. The ambassadors live there. So do various other dignitaries, civil servants and intelligentsia.

On one side, the Menteng area is bordered by the Thamrin boulevard, which boasts some of Indonesia's highest and most modern buildings. Less than 500 metres from this boulevard—but no longer in the fashionable Menteng area—lies Kebon Kacang, Nut Plantation, an interesting conglomeration of modern office buildings, private residences and slum dwellings.

Three Ursuline nuns (one US, two Indonesian) have a house here. They are actively involved in the life of the neighbourhood. They have education programmes for the women, hold classes for the children, and so on. First and foremost, they are good neighbours.

Sr Pauline noticed that one of the children seemed to be unable to keep up with the others at play. She seemed to have a slight deformity of the thigh. She took her to the polyclinic at the District Hospital some ten kilometres away, a long, hot journey on the Vespa scooter.

It transpired that the child was suffering from bone tuberculosis, most probably aggravated by bad housing (the whole family slept in a single dark room) and poor nutrition (85% of all children in Jakarta are malnourished).

Sr Pauline succeeded in getting the child admitted to the hospital. A team of doctors agreed to operate free of charge. Through social welfare, initial hospital and medicine bills were taken care of. When the child was eventually released from the hospital, she had to wear a cast on her thigh. This cast was not to be removed at any time until the next check-up. However, the cast proved to be a source of great amusement to the other children of the neighbourhood. They touched it and tore at it, greatly disconcerting the little girl. Nobody came to the rescue, and in her terror the child wetted herself. When Sr Pauline came by that evening, the cast was badly torn and smelled very unpleasant.

So the child had to be taken to the hospital once again to have the cast changed. The doctors told Sr Pauline that on no account was the cast to be removed, as it might cause permanent deformation of the thigh.

Sr Pauline told the child's parents to see to it that the cast remained in place and that the child didn't soil it. However, the parents both work all day. He's a garbage collector, she sells food at the market. Neither parent was able to protect the child from the harassment of other children. Some neighbours tried to do the best they could, but obviously this was not a satisfactory solution.

Sr Pauline tried, unsuccessfully, to get the child admitted to a children's home, an orphanage. She was told that there was no valid reason to accept the child, as it still had both parents living and a reasonably good home.

It wasn't until a journalist wrote an article on the child—in connection with the International Year of the Child—in Indonesia's leading newspaper *Sinar Harapan**, that Sr Pauline finally succeeded in getting the child admitted to the children's home. Perhaps she may not get the affection and the attention which the family may have given

* *Sinar Harapan*, "Ray of Hope" is a Christian (Protestant) newspaper, founded in 1962. From a small paper, it has grown into a major publishing concern, without ever having received aid from churches/missions overseas.

her—in those rare moments when the struggle for life's bare necessities did not take all their time and energy—but at least her thigh will have a better chance to heal.

CASE STUDY

Deprived child

Rosmala, a young girl in her teens, was employed at a massage parlour in one of Jakarta's fashionable hotels. For a fee, she could be persuaded to see the client after hours as well.

An attractive and fairly well-educated girl, she never had trouble getting customers. One of them, a middle-aged American engineer called Peter, eventually asked her to live with him for the length of his stay in Jakarta.

Rosmala left the massage-parlour and moved into Peter's room at the hotel. The management didn't object.

Peter asked her how she had come to work as a prostitute. Rosmala told him she came from a very poor family. Her mother was a domestic servant, and her father a repairman who was out of work most of the time. Being the eldest, she had to help out, giving most of her earnings to the family. She had learned how to deport herself and to speak passably good English by "picking it up from the other girls and a few kind customers".

When Peter's term of employment came to an end, he wanted to take Rosmala to the States with him, with a view to marrying her. She seemed to be quite agreeable, though not quite as enthusiastic as he would have supposed. She said she would come with him and give it a try for three months.

At the end of the three months, Peter had made up his mind to marry the girl. Rosmala, however, said she would have to return to Indonesia first to tell her parents.

Peter managed to get a new contract to Indonesia. As he felt slightly guilty at having taken away the family's main source of support, he prepared a food parcel and some gifts before they set out to meet Rosmala's family.

At Rosmala's insistence, they took the car. She directed it to one of the new residential areas of Jakarta, and to Peter's amazement, to a large mansion situated in a spacious garden. Bearing in mind that Rosmala's mother was a domestic servant, he asked whether they ought to use the back entrance.

Rosmala said it would be all right to go to the front door. She rang the bell. The door was opened by a servant who expressed great delight at seeing Rosmala.

"Is my mother at home?" the girl asked. The servant showed them to a sitting room, which in Peter's opinion seemed inordinately well-furnished and comfortable for the use of servants.

Presently, an impeccably dressed lady entered the room. She greeted Rosmala affably enough, and asked her what she had been doing lately, as she hadn't seen her since Idul Fitri the previous year.

"Why, mother," Rosmala said, "I met Peter here, and he took me to the States with him."

Peter volunteered the information that he wanted to marry Rosmala.

"Well, you'll have to ask her father about that," the mother said, "but you'll have to wait until he comes back. He's away on a business tour to Japan."

It transpired that Rosmala's parents were both highly educated and the family was obviously well-to-do. Rosmala had never lacked for any material or physical comfort in her life. Her parents had no idea of her occupation—when she failed to come home for days on end, they assumed that she was visiting friends or relatives.

When Peter asked Rosmala privately afterwards why she had not told him the truth, she said: "Well, I thought you would never believe me if I had told you the way things were: my father always away on business, my mother always wrapped up in socializing. Besides, when I told you I was doing it for a Good Cause, to save my family from starvation, you felt sorry for me!"

IV. Theological motifs

In preparing this chapter, I came across an article by the Dutch theologian Maria de Groot.[1] She called it "The Breakthrough of the Gospel in the Life of Women", and uses the story of the healing of the woman in Luke 13.

This woman was "bent double and quite unable to stand upright", besides being possessed by a spirit that left her enfeebled. Jesus laid his hands on her, and immediately she raised herself up. And she glorified God.

And that, says Maria de Groot, can only happen after you are raised up. "You can sing the prescribed song. You can participate in the community where only men have the leadership and can speak. But you do it as someone who is bent and distorted. Only if you are lifted up by the power of Jesus and in the space of the kingdom of God, then your own song awakens."

People often ask me why I am so concerned about the sexist language and sexist practices of the Church. What's wrong with calling God "Father", what's so tragic about women not being allowed to be ordained? The good work goes on anyway, and *that* is important, isn't it? Besides, my church has accepted women ministers almost from its inception, so why should I worry about other churches? In Indonesia, churches are distinct from one another not so much through denominational as ethnic and cultural factors. As a Minahassan woman, perhaps I should be aware of subtle differences in culture, and not poke my nose into relationships I don't understand.

Maria de Groot has said exactly what I would like to have said. As a woman, I too have felt bent and distorted. As a matter of fact, I still often feel that way.

And it is the power of Jesus which liberates woman, in the space of the Kingdom of God. So that woman can stretch herself to her full length, and glorify God.

Raising up woman

This is what it's all about: liberation, power, glorification. How good is the work which is being done by bent and distorted people within a structure that leaves them no room for "stretching to their full length"? Are we so fearful, have we so little confidence in the power of Christ and the

Kingdom of God, that we don't want all God's people stretching to their full length? Are we like the oppressors, who keep dangerous prisoners in tiger cages?

Maria de Groot also points out that, in Luke 13, the head of the synagogue really couldn't appreciate Jesus' healing the woman at all, as it was a sabbath day—and she sees a direct analogy with the attitude of today's church leaders, who are not overly enthusiastic either with "women on the sabbath and on Sundays, raised to their full height, taking the word and singing their own song, proclaiming from their own corporal recovery". In other words, they are very critical of women participating in salvation.

Jesus calls these spiritual leaders hypocrites, and throws the question right back at them: "If you free on the sabbath your ox and your donkey to let them drink, what then have you to say of my act regarding this woman? Is she not a daughter of Abraham?"

Jesus lifts up the woman to what she is. A daughter of Abraham, faced with the hypocrites who taught that they were the sons of Abraham. Yet who failed to grasp the essence of their own Torah. The woman is a daughter of Abraham, she does not have to become it by one or another achievement. For 18 years she has been bound by the power of evil—the power that Jesus calls Satan. And the hand of Christ is sufficient for complete liberation: there is no need for anything else. No approval of authorities, no proof from the woman's side. She is the daughter of Abraham, she is released.

And here I think of the words of another woman theologian, Nelle Morton: "While forgiveness must be permitted to bring its *shalom* into our lives, the *shalom* woman cannot do those whom she forgives the disservice of allowing them to remain in anti-shalom positions. While she loves and forgives the ones who sin against her, she can no longer permit the sins of sexism (and racism) to continue wherever they become identified."[2]

In the previous chapters it has already been pointed out that Asian women's self-image is less than satisfactory. In the case of Christian women, this poor self-image is preserved by the churches' tendency to give male chauvinism a theological and quasi-divine legitimation, so that there are churches where women have no awareness at all of being created in the image of God, *imago Dei*.

They are burdened by the thought that they are "the devil's gateway, who caused man, the image of God, to sin"—as Tertullianus so kindly stated, and some men are so fond of repeating.

At best, women are comforted by the thought of being a helper, something which is drummed into them at catechism lessons and wedding ceremonies. That *'ezer* in the Hebrew means "help" in the sense of mutual action, or the cooperation of subject and object where the strength of one is not sufficient,[3] seems to escape the good leaders' attention.

The importance of raising woman's awareness of her self-worth cannot be over-emphasized. Always accepting that God transcends all human understanding, we could make use here of the feminine aspects of divinity, and also of the meaning of the symbol of Mary, in order to restore woman's true image of herself. This is women's contribution to whole theology, which, as Nelle Morton says, "as full human experience, is only possible when all the oppressed peoples of the world can speak freely out of their own experiences, to be heard and touch one another to heal and be healed".[4]

The concept of God from the feminist perspective

A professor at a theological seminary in Indonesia once said to me in all seriousness: "Well, you can't deny it—God is male: just look at the way He is referred to as *He* throughout the Bible, with all the masculine forms of the verbs and nouns!"

Of course I could have answered that, if you look at things that way, you could also argue that God was Jewish, although a bit later in the stage of revelation, "He" also adopted a Greek garb and expressed "Himself" in a Hellenistic fashion—and whereas the people "He" had revealed "Himself" to were originally The Chosen People (i.e. the Jews), presently they came to include the Greeks. All *men*, of course, since after the Babylonian exile Jews had started to give thanks to the Lord for having created them as Jewish *men*, not Gentiles, slaves, or women;[5] and the Aristotelean concept of the human being was rather similar, only he thought of *Greeks* for *Hebrews*.

In the Indonesian language, as I have mentioned elsewhere, we don't have such a problem with pronouns, as "Dia" means both "he" and "she". Neither do we have such a fierce dichotomy as is evident in the West. My preoccupation with pronouns really started when I had to theologize in English, Dutch and German (in Swedish, God is "He", but *människa*—"human being"—is always "she"!), and I heartily sympathize with my western sisters. Language is, after all, where theology begins.

Anyway, my answer to the professor went like this. I asked him about the original meaning of *rechamim*, which is used for God's mercy, compassion (e.g. Exodus 34), He admitted that it literally means "movements of the *womb*" *(rechem)*.

Neither of us knew of any males who possessed wombs, so my professor was persuaded there might be a touch of the feminine here. This was, in my opinion, a Great Leap Forward, because browsing through Hebrew lexicons and the like, I found that some male theologians will perform the most extraordinary contortions exegetically in order to avoid relating *rechamim* to the feminine aspect of God.

I also asked how women could have been created in God's image if God was so decidedly male. And I pointed to the case of the Holy Spirit. The Third Person started out in Hebrew as the feminine *Ruach*, but was then effectively neutered by the Greek translators of the Septuaginta, then made masculine by Latin. Therefore, we are now blessed with an all-male Trinity. (We will return to the Spirit later.)

Thirdly, I asked whether there were no legitimate reasons for the old Hebrews to refer consistently to God as "He"—and did they *really* do that?

We must learn to read the Bible again. Over and against the masculine imagery—which does dominate the text —there are also feminine images which tend to be conveniently overlooked. We accept that the texts which have come to us are "the products of a society driven to choose male metaphors by virtue of patriarchal structures predicated upon sexual inequality", as Paul D. Hanson says.[6] We may still live in a society of patriarchal structures, but we flatter ourselves that there is no more sexual inequality.

In that context, one wonders why the name of God, Yahweh, which is a verb, not a noun, is still consistently translated as "Lord". This has been happening for centuries. To quote Dr Hanson again, it is "a conspiracy spanning three millennia". It is a fact that frequently the original texts make no indication of gender—this has been supplied gratuitously by translators.

It is true that—as we learned in our Hebrew language classes—the *Qetib*, or written form, is *Yahweh*, but the *Qere'*, or spoken form, is *Adonay*, which does mean "Lord". Even then, as a very young student in my first year at seminary, I thought it strange that one should write one thing and read another. At the time, I attributed this to my incomplete initiation into the higher theological mysteries. Now, of course, I relate it to something less high-faluting.

In her article "Over Psalm 1" (On Psalm 1), Maria de Groot, who is not only a theologian but also a linguist, draws our attention to the way the domination of male hyperboles and male symbols have seriously impaired revelation.

A hyperbole is an *over*-statement, like saying: "I'm absolutely starving", when one is slightly hungry. The opposite of hyperbole is litote, *under*-statement, like saying: "You're all right, you know," when one is actually deeply in love with that person. Maria de Groot claims that male hyperboles and female litotes have led many of us to believe that "male = God, therefore God = male". And what is female, then?

What is the metaphor for the righteous?

The polarization of male and female, she goes on to say, confuses the real issue. This is very clear in Psalm 1. It is not "male-female" which are contrasted, but rather—and rightly so—"righteous" and "wicked". They who delight in the law of God, over against those who don't.

The righteous is
  like a tree,
  planted beside a watercourse,
  which *yields its fruit* in season
  and its leaf never withers...

A very feminine symbol: "yielding fruit". And it is with this symbol that the righteous have been asked to identify themselves through the ages.

Of course, God is neither male nor female in an ontic sense. When we believe that women and men were created in God's image, we should remember that they were created together, as well as to complement one another. Servant-hood, not sexuality, is the primary bearer of God's image.[7]

In a previous chapter, I mentioned the fact that Mary is often overlooked as one of the women in Jesus' life, although one could rightly say that she is actually the first, and the most important. This is a typically Protestant idiosyncrasy.

A typically male chauvinist idiosyncrasy is under-emphasizing, or ignoring, the rich variety of metaphors in which Scripture refers to God in feminine images. We are all too well-acquainted with the images of Lord, King, Father, Ruler, and so on. But are we equally alert to the image of Mother, Comforter, Giver of Life?

In Deuteronomy 32:11 we read, for example:

As an eagle watches over its nest,
hovers about its young,
spreads its pinions and takes them up,
and carries them upon its wings.

Most of us have never seen a live eagle, so that we are not immediately sensitive to the mother-bird image that is presented here.

Since many of us have encountered live chickens, however, everyone will readily agree that nothing can be quite as protective as a mother-hen. So when Jesus cries out:

O Jerusalem, Jerusalem...
How often have I longed to gather your children
as a hen gathers her brood under her wings

a marvellous image of divine protectiveness is effortlessly conjured up in our minds.

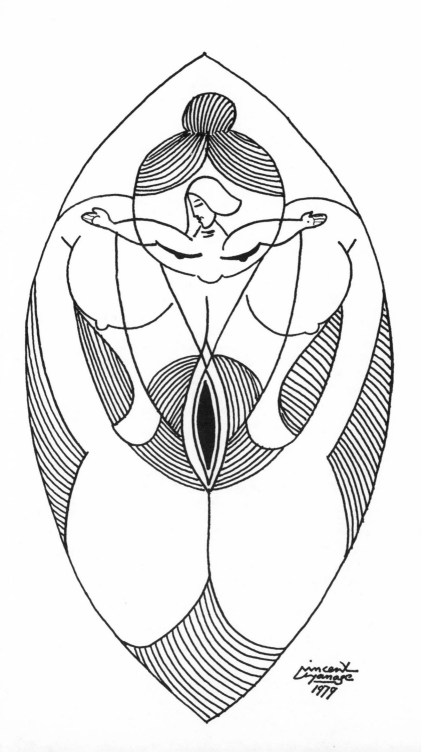

I have seen that the church buildings in Europe often symbolize the oppressive structures of medieval times in their architecture. (In Aachen, where German emperors used to be crowned, there is the Great Dom, cathedral, for the emperor and the aristocracy, and a few hundred meters further away there is the church for the common people.) In Suhl, German Democratic Republic, is a beautiful baroque church. It is quite large, and its various galleries and rooms are used for youth work. The pastor's young son has a little apartment high up in the belfry: two tiny rooms without heating, running water, or any "mod. cons", but with a marvellous view.

"Whatever gave you the idea to turn this belfry into living quarters?" I asked. "I only renovated it," the young man answered. "It used to be the Glockner's apartment—a family of five lived here as recently as the turn of the century!" While well-fed, well-clad, burghers were piously singing hymns downstairs, the Glockner—clock-keeper—and his family froze upstairs.

In Denpasar on the island of Bali, the church has been built in the traditional style, combined with Christian theological motifs. Tradition accounts for the pool in front of the church, and for the sculptures adorning the walls and doors. The roof of the church doesn't quite meet the walls. The space in between allows for adequate ventilation—Bali is a tropical island. Furthermore, this roof represents the image of God "hovering protectively" over the congregation.

The Balinese theologians who had thought this up looked rather taken aback when I remarked that this was a "motherly" image of God. Yet they saw nothing untoward in it. In Indonesia, the mother is very important. Also, the Balinese Church has ordained women ever since it began.

Childbirth is also an often employed form of imagery. If we insist on referring to God only in terms of "Father", no doubt we are uncomfortable when dealing with passages such as Deuteronomy 32:18:

You forsook the creator who begot you
and cared nothing for the God
who brought you to birth.

Or, for that matter, Isaiah 49:15:

Can a woman forget the infant at her breast,
or a loving mother the child of her womb?

God the Mother is really more common than we think. It is perhaps most clear in that beautiful passage in Hosea 11:

When Israel was a boy, I loved him.
I called my son out of Egypt,
but the more I called, the further they went from me.
...It was I who taught Ephraim to walk,
I who had taken them in my arms...
harnessed them in leading-strings
and led them with bonds of love.
...I lifted them like a little child to my cheek,
I had bent down to feed them.

And further on:

How can I give you up, Ephraim,
how surrender you, Israel?
My heart is changed within me,
my compassion grows warm and tender.

And in Isaiah 66:

As a mother comforts her son,
so will I myself comfort you.

Reference is also made here to "sucking, and being fed from the breasts that give comfort, delighting in the plentiful milk".

As James White pointed out, though anthropomorphisms abound in Scripture, usually even the faint suggestion of female anatomy for God troubles us.[8] Thus, in the prologue to John's Gospel, translators shy away from an exact rendition of the last verse (1:18), which says literally: "God's only begotten, he who is in the Father's *breast* (Greek: *kolpos*)". The New English Bible discreetly puts it as: "He who is nearest to the Father's *heart*."

When God is called Father, this is not to be taken in an ontic sense, i.e. it does not necessarily limit God to being male. Father is intended to express the loving concern of God who takes care of us. Here the category "father" is a symbol of divine fecundity and creativity.

The excessive emphasis on the maleness of God is seen by some as a reaction against the fertility goddesses of the Canaanite religious system. Although the dominant metaphor in this cult was feminine, it reduced woman to a sex object, as is amply illustrated by the fertility plaques with their exaggerated representations of the breasts and genitalia. This is something which we will have to bear in mind constantly in our search for a whole image of God.

Again, Asians may look at the other religions. In the meta-cosmic soteriologies of Asia, such as Hinduism, it is unthinkable to dichotomize male and female to the extent the Christian West has done, any more than it is possible to dichotomize life and death.

The oppression of an all-male Trinity

The Borobudur is a world-famous temple in central Java. Built in the seventh century A.D., it is a Shiva-Buddhist shrine. Although it is structured in the form of a *stupa*, adorned with statues of the Lord Buddha and reliefs of his life, it is also replete with *lingams*, which are symbols of the Lord Shiva.

In high school, during cultural history classes, the teacher off-handedly explained that the *lingam* was a phallic symbol. We dutifully copied down this information in our notebooks, without having the slightest idea what the symbol stood for, as none of us knew either Sanskrit or Latin.

Actually, every *lingam* stands on a base called the *yoni*, which symbolizes the female organ. The whole thing was a fertility symbol, and whoever was responsible for building the Borobudur was sufficiently cognizant of the facts of life not to ascribe fertility to one sex only.

In the primal (or cosmic) religions of Asia, people have worshipped their ancestors—not just a male father. In the cult of the Rice Mother, who is still venerated throughout the Indonesian archipelago, people also worship her spouse.[9]

I find Hinduism most interesting. The *Sakti*, the feminine aspect of the deity, is by no means subordinate or inferior to the deity, she *is* the Deity. "Durga, or Kali, is the Sakti, the goddess of power, the spouse of and energy for Shiva, who is the god of pure consciousness."[10]

Durga is also the goddess of death. The oldest temple in Bali is perched on a steep promontory hundreds of meters over the Indonesian Ocean, of which she is believed to be the queen. Durga's statue, which must be over a thousand years old, is almost worn smooth. How can people worship a goddess of death with such devotion? Because she is also the goddess of life, activity, energy, power. Life and death are one.

Forcing people to relate to an all-male Trinity is oppression. In the context of Asian cosmic religion and metacosmic soteriologies, it is also ridiculous.

The Holy Spirit

In the tradition of the ecclesiastical West, the Holy Spirit is *He*. As I have already pointed out, this is due to the fact that the feminine *Ruach* of the Hebrew was first effectively neutered by the good fathers of the Septuaginta, then made masculine for good measure by the Latin. And it goes without saying that Aristotelean thinking ("man" not being a generic, but meaning "a free, Greek, *male*") also exerted a great amount of undue influence.

Is it coincidence that the symbol for the Holy Spirit is the dove? In Greek this word is *peristerà*, which means "Bird of Ishtar", the virgin goddess whom we already have discussed earlier.

Is it so far-fetched to think that the battle between Yahweh (supposedly male) and Ishtar (definitely female) still seems to be going on?[11]

Somewhere along the line, it was apparently decreed that the Trinity should be all male. Hence the adoration of the Virgin Mary as "daughter of the Father, mother of Jesus, *spouse* of the Holy Spirit". A perfect example of the way some men would like to see women: always as daughter/mother/spouse, never as a human being in her own right. And Mary, the virgin in the primal sense of the word, becomes the dutifully domesticated symbol of that which she is *not*.

In view of the quality and the function of the Spirit as God who creates, who comforts, "the Giver of Life" (as the Nicene Creed says), it is not surprising that the Gnostic writings, such as the Gospel of the Hebrews and the Acts of Thomas, called the Holy Spirit explicitly "*Mother* of Jesus, *Mother* of all creatures".

Of course, these writings are not canonical. As a matter of fact, they may be considered heretical. This is a symptom which is often sighted in history, more especially Church history. Whoever begged to differ was usually in for a sorry fate—like the Montanists, who gave great prominence to the Spirit, and who ordained women. We all know what terrible and perverted creatures they were from the writings which have come down to us. Not *their* writings, to be sure, but the treatises which good and true Christians wrote against the Montanists' horrible heresies.

In this connection, one wonders how Luther or Calvin would have fared, if the only source we had of their lives and teachings was the official Vatican version of the time.

This insistence that the three persons are all male has led to some complications.

In one Pakistani language, the word for Spirit is feminine. However, thanks to the Nicene Creed calling the Spirit Lord, as the English liturgical texts also do, this language had to be changed: the natural idiom ceased to exist, and in its place the people got "translationese", or perhaps it would be more accurate to say here "religionese". How wonderful. More than ever Christians will have an awareness of being a people that has been set apart, if even their language is unintelligible except to a select few.

The Spirit, who goes where She wills, is the first of the Three Persons to be reified (made to be a thing). The whole *filioque* controversy should make this clear.

From God, the Spirit became a thing. Eventually, She was regarded as "the monopolistic possession of the Judaeo-Christian tradition imprisoned within the steel and concrete structures of· western dogma and a permanent Atlantic Charter."[12]

The best illustration I ever saw of this point was in Taizé's Church of the Reconciliation, to which we were taken during the 1978 Bossey Graduate School of Ecumenical Studies.

Kneeling in a church which was so dark that I had an atavistic sense of being back in the womb, I saw something white moving in the flickering lights of the altar. When I went up after the service to have a closer look, I realized it was a white dove in a cage—put there to symbolize the Holy Spirit, as I was told.

I went out of the church much saddened by what we do to the Spirit in the darkness of our minds and the narrowness of our thinking.

Is it heresy to say that the Spirit sings to us in the *Bhagavad Gita*, the Song of God, or dances for us in Lord Shiva's dance, or speaks to us in the words of the Enlightened One? If so, why is it all right to send small children out into the garden early in the morning to look for Easter eggs—a custom connected with a forgotten spring goddess called Ostara? How is it possible that the Christmas tree has become such an established symbol of Christianity that political parties (for example, the now dissolved Parkindo, Indonesian Christian Party) have used it as their emblem? There are very few people in Europe today who remember that the origin of the Christmas tree was in the heathen legend of Odin, Father of the Gods, who vowed to destroy the world when the last leaf had fallen. As the fir tree does not shed its leaves, the world was saved. Boniface was able—and allowed—to transform this piece of pagan practice into a ritual that Christians all over the world go through now every year, no doubt to the great delight of manufacturers of Christmas cards and other trimmings.

The very essence of the Spirit is "boundless freedom". It follows that to put any limits on the Spirit's activity is to negate that freedom. This doesn't mean that there are no discernible signs to recognize the Spirit's continuing work.

As Stanley Samartha says, the Spirit means life (vitality, creativity, growth), not death. Order (meaning, significance, truth), not chaos. Community (sharing, fellowship, bearing one another's burden), not separation.

Wherever these marks are found, there one should sense the work of the Spirit.

To me this is expressed very movingly in the poem which one of my fellow-students, Sally Dyck, wrote for the Graduate School of Ecumenical Studies at Bossey last year. The poem starts like this:

Transforming womb of God
conceive in us.
Create anew life:
    Faith, the confidence to bear
    Hope, continuously expectant
    Love, the true beginning.

Oikoumene isn't limited

I remember a case which deeply disturbed me at the time, as it really challenged my understanding of the Spirit and of ecumenism.

Oikoumene as I understand it isn't just the more or less reluctant agreement of Christians to share the same church building, the same liturgy or even the same eucharist. It is more than that, since our *oikoumene* really isn't just limited to Christians, but consists of all human beings: people of all living faiths, cultures and ideologies.

In 1975, I was working with the Karo Batak Christian community in Jakarta, in my pastoral training course. Most of the members of the congregation were people who had left their Karo homeland for the first time in their lives, and found it difficult to adjust to the sudden transition to a metropolis like Jakarta. Future shock, culture shock, and of course ecumenical shock. From small villages where everybody was of the same lineage and of the same faith, they were suddenly transplanted into a place where diversity was the rule.

A family of three, father, mother and teenage son, lived in such a situation. They were the only Bataks in the place where they had settled. They were also the only Christians. Nevertheless, they got along very well with their neighbours.

Once, the parents were away from home for a few days. They were traders and often had to travel. During their absence, their son had an accident and died.

As the dead have to be buried within 24 hours in tropical countries, the neighbours got together and gave the boy a decent burial. Muslim, of course, with the appropriate prayers and readings from the Quran by the Muslim priest.

When the parents returned, their grief was compounded by some good Christians assuring them that now their son was sure to burn in hell, because he had not been buried properly, by a Christian pastor.

I was asked my opinion. All I could say was that we are not saved by the soil we are buried in, or the words which are mumbled over us at birth or in death. We are saved by the blood of Christ.

How typically "Christian", I thought, to turn this gesture of comfort into yet another burden of grief for the bereft parents—to read this sign and this promise of the Spirit as a sure sign of damnation. This first tentative step by Muslims towards ecumenism was construed by some Christians as an act of imposition.

Perhaps we need more wisdom as we try to understand the Spirit and Her great work.

Hokmah and Shekinah

For a more relevant women's theology, it would be useful to reflect a little more on the significance of other feminine aspects of divinity. Besides *Ruach*, the Old Testament presents us with *Hokmah* (wisdom) and *Shekinah* (presence).

Hokmah had the good fortune to remain feminine in the "sacred" languages (Greek: *sophia*, Latin: *sapientia*), a fact which I found extremely interesting, as women are often accused of lacking in wisdom.[13]

As for *Shekinah*, perhaps the following passage illustrates her importance: "A heathen asked Rabbi Joshua ben Kaska: 'Why did God speak to Moses from the thorn bush?'

"Rabbi Joshua replied, 'If He had spoken from a carob tree or a sycamore, you would have asked me the same question! But so as not to dismiss you without an answer, God spoke from the thorn bush to teach you that there is no place where the *Shekinah* is not, not even a thorn bush."[14]

We have already mentioned briefly some images relating to the motherliness of God in the Old Testament, but there are many other such images elsewhere. The Church Fathers were generally very misogynic in their outlook, for reasons which need not immediately concern us here. Yet Clement of Alexandria sings,

God is Love
God can only be perceived in love.
Father in his inexpressible being,
Mother in his compassionate pity for us.
In his love for us
The Father became woman.
The great sign for us is this:
He who was born.

Clement has the deep insight of the ecstatic love for Christ in the Early Church when, as Karl Rahner remarked somewhat wistfully, theologians were still poets and able to see the greater context. However, Eulogia Würz points out that it is not quite right to say that only "in his love for us" God became woman. God is Father and Mother in all eternity.[15]

Then consider Anselm of Canterbury, who wrote in 1093:
"And Thou, Jesus, sweet Lord, art Thou not also a mother? Truly, Thou art a mother, the mother of all mothers, Who tasted death, in Thy desire to give life to Thy children."

Maria de Groot comments that the words of Anselm are "(those) of a theologian on the way of prayer, who discovers the secret of birth and death which is as male as it is female, in the person of Jesus, the giver of life. Anselm experiences being mother and woman as a reality which gives life and reconciles."

Even Pope John Paul I referred to God as Our Father-Mother.

There is nothing new or strange in acknowledging the motherliness of God. Yet why do so many apparently still recoil at the thought?

In Indian devotional literature of the *bhakti* school, God is often spoken of as "Mother", for it is felt that the love of a mother for her child is one of the highest and most unselfish forms of human love. Hindus therefore find it strange that the Christian tradition does not speak of God in this way, and sometimes draw attention to the fact that the Roman Catholic cult of the Virgin Mary is perhaps an attempt to compensate, giving scope to that side of human nature which longs for the comfort that a mother can give.

The Indian poet Narayan Vaman Tilak wrote of Christ:

Tenderest Mother-Guru mine,
Saviour, where is love like thine?

Again I refer to the custom some tribes in Indonesia have to call the bride-giving (i.e. the mother's clan) "the visible God". And to the Quranic saying: "Paradise is under the sole of mother's feet."

Dr Shoki Coe drew my attention to the fact that the Chinese character for surname 姓 has "woman" and "bone" as its radicals. "Bone of the woman"—again, the mother, is the most important.

In developing an Asian theology, we must never underestimate her importance.

V. Women in Asian theology

There are many images that cross my mind as I write this chapter. I see a woman sitting in a busy street in Colombo, among other souvenir sellers. She looks tired, and doesn't praise her wares to passers-by as loudly as her colleagues. Or perhaps one should say, her rivals. Across her lap lies a sleeping child.

Then there is another image: of a woman, no longer young, waiting outside an elite hotel. A man comes out carrying a trash can, which he empties in front of her. She goes through the refuse meticulously, and manages to retrieve a few items which are of value to her.

I also see a woman carrying a small child covered with sores. She lives in a shanty settlement which is called *Kampung Plastik* (the Plastic Village). It got its name because the inhabitants, chiefly street-walkers, built their homes out of plastic sheets and bags which they had collected at a building site rubbish heap. The woman tells us the child's sores don't heal, although she has tried everything. What does "everything" mean, when she doesn't even have access to running water? She has to buy her drinking water, as the village is too near the sea to have natural fresh water. Besides, from the look of it, the nun beside me tells me the child probably has congenital syphilis.

I think of the young domestic servant, who accidentally burned her mistress's dress while ironing. The gentle lady was so annoyed that she poured scalding hot water over the girl, and then had her doctor husband abandon her in the cemetery.

Then there is the woman who gave birth to twins in the middle of Calcutta, near the garbage cans in a busy street. Too weak to lift herself up, she could not do anything to defend her babies when the dogs came and devoured them.

There are many more women whom I would like you to meet. The worker in the tea-plantation. The woman who toils in a stone quarry all day. The laundry woman who has slaved all her life to educate her two daughters, and finds that one is now overqualified and the other has turned to prostitution. The textile-factory workers who are subjected to inhuman treatment, of which the least appalling is having excrement rubbed into their face, simply because they ask for equal rights. The toy factory worker who cannot afford a toy for her own child.

And there is also the bourgeois woman with a good income (either from her husband or from her own job) who fails to understand why we civilized Asians should "follow this decadent western Women's Lib". She goes to church and says her prayers—isn't that enough?

Eucharist

I have always found it difficult to celebrate the eucharist, or Holy Communion, or whatever we call it. How can we sit in beautiful big buildings, eating and drinking from silver plates and chalices, "in remembrance of" Jesus, who presumably never owned a house or silver utensils? That was the question I used to ask my Sunday school teacher. I could never figure out just exactly what it was Jesus had died for, if this was the way we commemorated him. Wouldn't it be better to feed the hungry and heal the sick as he had done?

Eucharist, my seminary professor would tell me, means grace, joy, thanksgiving, for God's self-giving love. A very wonderful and exalted thing. In Indonesia, many churches have the custom of preparing the table in the shape of the cross. It was considered more proper to wear black, and of course an appropriately gloomy face—which did not reveal much of the joy and thanksgiving.

The eucharist is considered such a sacred rite that many women feel unworthy to partake of it during their period. In such a context, one can understand why some churches hesitate to ordain women as priests, who would not only partake, but also actually serve the sacraments.

Is the eucharist no more than that—just a rite for which one has to attain a certain level of purity? Very exclusive?

In the oldest New Testament account, I Corinthians 11, we read of people being unable to eat the Lord's Supper, "because each of you is in such a hurry to eat his own, and while one goes hungry another has too much to drink". And Paul goes on to say: "Are you so contemptuous of the Church of God that you shame its poorer members? What am I to say? Can I commend you? On this point, certainly not!"

In Luke's version (chapter 22), we get the impression that the context of the eucharist is the whole political problem of those who set themselves over against one another. Jesus' inviting his disciples to the Last Supper was a foretaste of the heavenly banquet, where such disputes should be no more, serving one another.

In the Church, the eucharist should be the visible means of breaking through socio-economic barriers, as it was in the life of the early Christians. Instead of accentuating such barriers, the Church should bring a eucharistic meaning to the broken life. As expressed in Revelations 19, "the fine linen signifies the righteous deeds of God's people".

When women cannot serve the eucharist—when certain people feel ashamed because they cannot come to the table in the proper attire, when there is bickering about the ingredients to be used: may one use lime juice and cassava, or should one "faithfully" stick to European wine and bread?—what is the eucharist then?

The eucharist is a sign. Instead of spending too much time polishing and upgrading the sign, perhaps Christians should reflect on what it stands for, and in which direction it is pointing. Whether it communicates inclusive or exclusive being.

As Father Tissa Balasuriya remarked, Jesus celebrated the eucharist only once, and within 48 hours he was dead, killed by the oppressive social structures he sought to liberate people from.[1]

That is the true context of the eucharist.

The theology of the womb

It is becoming more and more clear in Asia that the hope of salvation—conceived in terms both of this world and the world to come—is the chief concern of humanity's religious quest[2]—salvation no longer meaning the abandonment of this world in favour of the world to come, but rather the involvement in the struggle for peace and freedom.

History is not a thing that continuously repeats itself, crushing us remorselessly as it goes. History has to do with people: it is people who shape history, who are part of the power that gives birth to history.

We are the people, and we have a responsibility to fulfil ourselves in the passage of time. Our duty is to ensure the continuation of life, without which history is meaningless. In this perspective we should see the great emphasis which the people of Asia place on the continuation of family life, and the Asian outlook on salvation, closely related as it is to the experience of life in the mother's womb.

When the family is seen as only related to modes of production, which seems to be the attitude in certain circles in the West, it is not surprising that it is disintegrating; some people predict it will have ceased to exist by the year 2000-and-something. However, this is not the case in most parts of Asia. As I have mentioned in the previous chapters, the ties of kinship are still very strong and blood is definitely thicker than water.

Life is not simply "my life"—it is part of the life of all others before me, pressing on towards the future.

C.S. Song quotes a moving poem by a South Vietnamese poet, describing the grief and hope of a young wife who has just received the news of her husband's death in battle:

In confusion she looks down
at the seed coming to life in her
coming to the misery of life
try to grow up like your father, my darling.[3]

Song goes on to say: "For Asians, the concentration of human hope is in the womb, where past, present and future converge. Such a hope is historical, existential and eschatological. Hope is inseparably bound with the continuation of life from one generation to another.

"Creation, apprehended in the perspective of redemption, is the true foundation of human community, in which begins the kingdom of God, that links all humanity in a common kinship and blood relationship."

Conclusion

One of my Asian friends said to me: "Why should *you* of all people write a book on Asian women's theology? You are more westernized than Asian, in my opinion."

"Look who's talking," I retorted, stung to the quick. "You speak English, you have collected several degrees at western universities, you don't exactly wear traditional *sarong*, you live in a western style house and drive a German car... Aren't *you* westernized?"

"Well, of course, it's different for *men*," he said, genuinely surprised.

NOTES

CHAPTER I

[1] Tissa Balasuriya, OMI:. *The Eucharist and Human Liberation*. Colombo: Centre for Society and Religion, 1975, p. 45.

[2] Emanuel Lévinas: *La révélation*. Brussels: Facultés universitaires Saint-Louis, 1977.

[3] Those who are interested may read, for example, the works of Emanuel Lévinas or Enrique Dussel.

[4] Enrique Dussel: *Ethics and the Theology of Liberation*. Maryknoll, NY: Orbis Books, 1975, pp. 14-15.

CHAPTER II

[1] It has been pointed out that Tribuanottunggadewi—"Lady of the Three Worlds"—the mother of Majapahit's most famous king, Hayam Wuruk, ruled as Regent *not* for her son, but for her mother Gayatri, who had become a contemplative nun. In the year of Gayatri's death, Hayam Wuruk also came of age. Most western historians have misinterpreted Tribuanottunggadewi's relinquishing the throne at that particular moment in history as her having been a regent during her son's minority.

[2] A miscellaneous writer, whose best-known article is "A Vindication of the Rights of Women" (1792). She died a few days after having given birth to her second child, Mary Godwin, who later achieved fame as Mary Shelley, wife of the poet and creator of *Frankenstein*.

[3] Cf. M. Esther Harding: *Woman's Mysteries, Ancient and Modern*. London, New York: Longmans, Green & Co., 1936.

[4] James Frazer: *The Golden Bough*. New York and London: Macmillan Co., 1917.

[5] Aloysius Pieris, SJ: "From Lilies to Roses". *Outlook*, Vol. 3, No. 6, 1971.

[6] Ivan Illich, when he asked to be released from the priesthood, also asked to be allowed to keep his vow of celibacy.

[7] Aloysius Pieris, SJ, *op. cit.*

CHAPTER III

[1] Aloysius Pieris, SJ: "Towards an Asian Teology of Liberation: Some Religio-cultural Guidelines." Paper presented at the Asian Theological Conference, Wennapuwa, Sri Lanka, 1979.

[2] August Bebel: *Die Frau und der Sozialismus*, 25th ed., 1895.

[3] See "Sexual Exploitation in a Third World Setting." Paper by Mary John Mananzan, OSB, to be published by CTC-CCA.

[4] Susan Brownmiller: *Against Our Will*. New York: Penguin Books, 1975, p. 14.

[5] See "Sexual Exploitation in a Third World Setting", *op. cit.*

[6] Cf. Frances FitzGerald: *Fire in the Lake*. As quoted by C. S. Song: *Third Eye Theology*. Maryknoll, NY: Orbis Books, 1979, chapter 6.

[7] *Beyond God the Father*. Boston: Beacon Press, 1975.

[8] Joyce Goldman: ''The Women of Bangla Desh,'' *Ms.*, 1 August 1972, p. 84.

CHAPTER IV

[1] In *Newsletter*, No. 3, WSCF Women's Project. Geneva, March 1979.

[2] *The Shalom Woman*, ed. Margaret Wold. Minneapolis, Minn.: Augsburg Publishing House, 1975.

[3] See Jenni/Westermann: *Theologisches Handwörterbuch zum Alten Testament*, Vol. II. Munich: Chr. Kaiser, 1976.

[4] *Op. cit.*

[5] Tosepta.

[6] "Masculine Metaphors for God and Sex Discrimination in the Old Testament." *The Ecumenical Review*, Vol. 27, No. 4, October 1975.

[7] Erminie Huntress Lantero: *The Feminine Aspects of Divinity*. Wallingford, Penn.: Pendle Hill, 1973.

[8] "The Words of Worship, Beyond Liturgical Sexism." *The Christian Century*, 13 December 1978.

[9] Cf. Philip van Akkeren: *Sri and Christ*. London: Lutterworth Press, 1970.

[10] T. K. Thomas: "India's Test-Tube Baby." *One World*, March 1979.

[11] Cf. Gerhard Voss: "Maria in der Feier des Kirchenjahres." *Una Sancta*, No. 4, 1977, pp. 308-309.

[12] S. J. Samartha: "The Holy Spirit and People of Various Faiths, Cultures and Theologies." *The Holy Spirit*, ed. Dow Kirkpatrick. Nashville, Tenn.: Tidings, 1974.

[13] Post-exilic literature shows how *Hokmah* (eventually *Shekinah*) was almost personified: "A female form of great refinement and beauty, whose utterances were most profound and radiant." She inspired love. She *was* love. Just take a look at the Proverbs, the Book of Wisdom, Jesus Sirach—whenever *Hokmah* was the subject, even the most dessicated hagiographer would wax lyrical in praise of her (cf. Eulogia Würz: "Das Mütterliche in Gott." *Una Sancta*, No. 4, 1977). In the light of the New Covenant, rather than personifying Wisdom, shouldn't we see *Hokmah* as God's personal inclination to the world, as the form in which God is with us, and wants to be sought by us? It is interesting also to note that in the Early Church there seems to have been an identification of *Hokmah* with Jesus.

[14] C. G. Montefiore and H. Loew: *A Rabbinic Anthology*. New York: Macmillan, 1938.

[15] *Op. cit.*

CHAPTER V

[1] *The Eucharist and Human Liberation*, op. cit.

[2] C. S. Song: *Third Eye Theology*, op. cit.

[3] Ngoyen Ngoc Binh, ed.: *A Thousand Years of Vietnamese Poetry*. New York: Alfred A. Knopf, 1975.

Appendices

POWER AND AUTHORITY:
UNITY OF WOMEN AND MEN IN THE THAI TRADITION

KOSON SRISANG

The traditional vision of the world by which my people live and act is at once cosmological and historical. That is to say, space and time are the two most important categories. Accordingly, an authentic person is one who, as one of our sayings goes, "knows time and space". A good action, therefore, is the human response to the fullness of time and space.

The categories of time and space correspond to the categories of power and authority, female and male. But the most important thing is not the fact of distinction; rather, it is the fundamental unity between the pairs. In short, time and space, power and authority, female and male are two sides of the same coin. Together they constitute unity, wholeness, authenticity and communion.

The real question, then, is this. What are the dynamics of this unity, wholeness, authenticity and communion? From the perspective of my tradition, the answer is to be found in another pair of categories, namely, freedom and compassion. Again two sides of the same coin. For one can be truly free when one is truly compassionate, and vice versa.

The best illustration of this vision of the Thai tradition is the following. The word for "commander in chief of the armed forces" is *mae thap*, which means "the *mother* of the armed forces". Indeed, there were times in our history when the *mae thap* were, in fact, female. But from the records, they were and still are mostly male. But the word is *mae* or mother. Why?

In order to understand this riddle we must return to the original vision of the Thai world which, as stated above, is at once cosmological and historical. With regard to cosmology, our world consists of the sun, the sky, the earth, the king, the army, the people, and all other beings. The archtypical relationship of these constituents of the world is that of male and female, of husband and wife, i.e. the sun is male in relation to the sky; the sky is male in relation to the earth; the earth is male in relation to the king; the king is male in relation to his people; etc. That is to say, each of the constituents, for example the king, is at once male and female in the context of the entire world. The commander in chief or the *mae thap* is therefore *female* in relation to the king and *male* in relation to those under his/her command. The truth about this word, *mae thap*, therefore is the unity of women and men.

Following this vision history is the realization, in part or in full, of the human search for wholeness and communion, inspired by the power of freedom and compassion, consummated in the communion of the female and the male dimensions of the human being.

Geneva, 31 May 1979

APPENDIX II
LANGUAGE

The word *wanita* lends itself nicely to the lyrics of songs and poems. That dulcet descriptions may actually have an insidious effect on people's way of thinking, is not always immediately obvious.

It has been noted that there has been an increasing tendency to use complicated Sanskrit loan-words instead of the simple, straightforward Malay.

This was the case with the term *pelacur*, for example. It means "someone who sells *(melacur)* him/herself"; in other words, *a prostitute* (male or female).

Today, the term *Wanita Tuna Susila*—abbreviated WST—is widely accepted. Literally, it means "woman without morals". *Tuna* always indicates "a lack of, being devoid of", e.g. *tuna netra* (without eyes, i.e. blind), *tuna karya* (without work, i.e. unemployed), *tuna wisma* (without house, i.e. homeless). Notice that there is no corresponding term *pria tuna susila*: "*man* without morals".

In tribal societies*, it is interesting to note the different ways of addressing women.

In the Batak societies, which are patriarchal, the words used for *wife* usually have a derogatory meaning. True, the mother of the house is called *inanta soripada* which implies great respect. However, a Karo Batak husband may call his wife *diberu tukur*, literally meaning "the bought woman". This reflects the bride-price the family had to pay to get this woman (see the chapter on socio-political realities). He could also call her "she, who feeds my pigs", or "my chattel".

In the Minahassa, a wife is referred to by her husband as *karya*, "friend"; or he might call her "she, who *shares* my kitchen".

It has been contended that the position of women in Indonesia was actually *good*, speaking generally, until the advent of colonialism. It cannot be denied that the adoption of bourgeois values has in many instances resulted in the subordination of women.

In the past, for example, a Javanese woman might have retained her own name. In the working class stratum, she still does. If Pujiati were to marry Suwirya, they would still be called Pujiati and Suwirya. However, in the educated middle class, she would prefer to be called Mrs Kartono.

In Bali, if her eldest child was called Putu, she would be called *Men Putu* (Mother of Putu), and her husband would be *Pan Putu* (Putu's father). Again, in the educated middle class, she would be Mrs Suwirya. Her identity is defined and absorbed by that of her husband.

In Indonesia, the formal word for addressing a man is still *tuan*, which really means "Lord". *The* Lord, i.e. God, is *Tuhan*, with an aspirated *h*. In itself, the word is neither male nor female, but like all Malay nouns/pronouns has to be qualified to the gender. Hence, an Indonesian feminist theologian would find less difficulty than her western sisters in relating to the Deity, *He* Who is *Lord*, because in Bahasa Indonesia *dia* (third personal pronoun) and *tuhan* would not be so categorically *male*.

The word *tuan* is being discarded, on account of its implications of class

---

* To those who are allergic to the words "tribal" or "tribe", I wish to say that it is used here to denote "a group of persons forming a community and claiming descent from a common ancestor", and also "a division from some other nation or people".

inequality. President Soekarno's Saudara—"brother/sister"*—although widely used, is giving way to the more natural form of address to a man one's senior (seniority implying superiority), i.e. *Bapak*, "father".

Whether he were a president, a cardinal or a garbage collector, the acceptable way of addressing a man would invariably be *Bapak*, regardless of age or civil status.

The same applies to *Ibu*, "Mother". Personally, I feel this is far preferable to the terms *Nyonya* (Mrs) and *Nona* (Miss), which are not original Malay, but of Portuguese origin.

---

* Note that *saudara* (sa + udara) literally means "(of) one womb". It may be applied to cousins. To show that one is referring to full brothers/sisters, the adjective *Kandung* (again meaning womb) is added.

APPENDIX III

WOMEN AS OBJECTS

AN AIRLINE POWERED BY CHARM — this is the first part of the caption to a colour photograph of three air hostesses near the engine of a Boeing 747. The caption continues: FLYING HIGH WITH THE SINGAPORE GIRLS.

"Many airlines have tried to sell the notion that they have something unique to offer, and not many have succeeded. One that did is the flag carrier for the minuscule Southeast Asian nation of Singapore. Singapore Airlines thrives on Oriental charm, mainly the charm of its exotic cabin hostesses—Chinese, Malays, Indians and Eurasians—who dress in sultry versions of the Malay *sarong kabaya*, designed by Pierre Balmain, and bewitch passengers with warm smiles, cool moist towels, and copious attention. They ply even economy class passengers with gifts, exquisitely prepared food, free cocktails, and free French wines and brandy. On long night flights, some first class passengers get tucked between the sheets on six couches that are converted into full-length beds.

"To complement its eastern graciousness, the airline looks West for its flying machines and most of its chief pilots. The combination of gentleness and efficiency helps the airline lure customers from competitors on routes that now span half the globe. SIA, as it is generally called, flies with an average of 74% of its passenger seats filled—the highest load factor of *any* major scheduled international carrier.

"Wooing customers with a touch of Asian sex appeal made Pillay (SIA chairman) uneasy at first. But Lim, the managing director, wanted SIA to have what he terms "a brand identity", to project the image of Singapore itself—"modern and progressive, but not entirely divorced from the romance of the East". Lim figured that marketing SIA as competent and modern would make it a "me, too" airline. So he went for the romance.

"A gently persuasive, but effective, advertising campaign glamourizes the cabin hostess as "the Singapore girl"—and helps the airline attract more than three million passengers a year.

". . . The campaign is not entirely candid, since about half the cabin attendants are men, but there is no doubt that it has worked. To convey the idea of in-flight pleasure with a lyrical quality, most SIA ads are essentially large colour photographs of various hostesses. In a broadcast commercial that sounds like a Burt Bacharach ballad, a crooner sings: "Singapore girl, you look so good I want to stay up here with you forever."

". . . The Singapore girls spend more time with customers than anyone else in the company does, and are its most effective sales force. Far from being repelled by the notion of becoming a "girl", about 7,000 young Singaporean women last year applied for 347 openings in the hostess ranks.

". . . Rather than staging a beauty contest, Lim says he looks for "the open simple type of girl whom we can make sophisticated in our way". He has the time to spend on such niceties. "I sometimes pity my colleagues in other airlines", Lim says, "because they are preoccupied with public-relations battles against criticism and fighting for support of governments and unions".

". . . Many places around the world will soon have their first encounters with the Singapore girl: China, East Africa, Latin America.

". . . Given a reasonable chance to compete; the airline should be able to persuade a lot more passengers to stay up there, as the song says, with those Singapore girls."

(Louis Kraar in Fortune Magazine, *18 June 1979)*